A World of Cats
to Color

Willow Bascom

ISBN 9781792965548
Independently published
Plymouth, Vermont

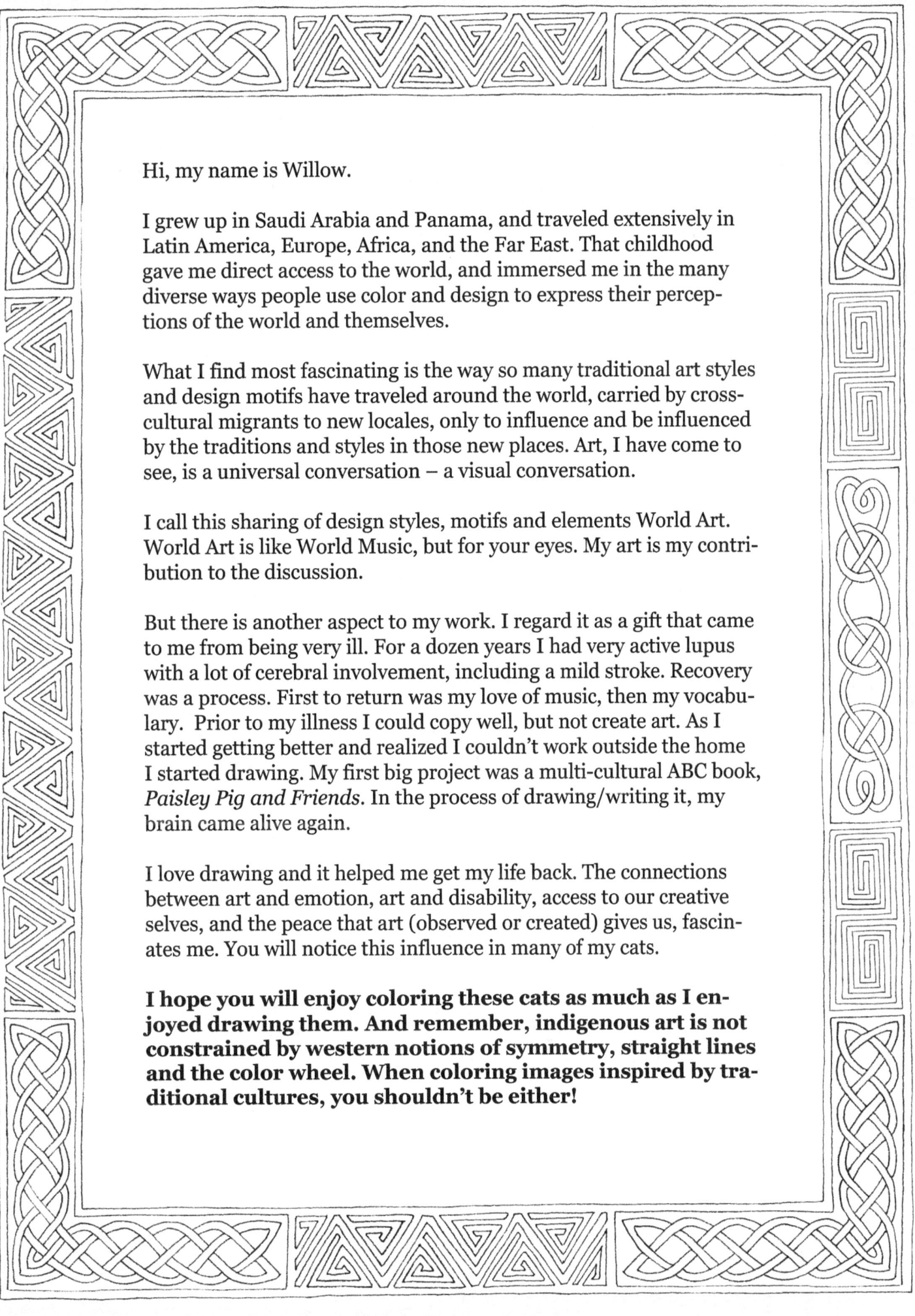

Hi, my name is Willow.

I grew up in Saudi Arabia and Panama, and traveled extensively in Latin America, Europe, Africa, and the Far East. That childhood gave me direct access to the world, and immersed me in the many diverse ways people use color and design to express their perceptions of the world and themselves.

What I find most fascinating is the way so many traditional art styles and design motifs have traveled around the world, carried by cross-cultural migrants to new locales, only to influence and be influenced by the traditions and styles in those new places. Art, I have come to see, is a universal conversation – a visual conversation.

I call this sharing of design styles, motifs and elements World Art. World Art is like World Music, but for your eyes. My art is my contribution to the discussion.

But there is another aspect to my work. I regard it as a gift that came to me from being very ill. For a dozen years I had very active lupus with a lot of cerebral involvement, including a mild stroke. Recovery was a process. First to return was my love of music, then my vocabulary. Prior to my illness I could copy well, but not create art. As I started getting better and realized I couldn't work outside the home I started drawing. My first big project was a multi-cultural ABC book, *Paisley Pig and Friends*. In the process of drawing/writing it, my brain came alive again.

I love drawing and it helped me get my life back. The connections between art and emotion, art and disability, access to our creative selves, and the peace that art (observed or created) gives us, fascinates me. You will notice this influence in many of my cats.

I hope you will enjoy coloring these cats as much as I enjoyed drawing them. And remember, indigenous art is not constrained by western notions of symmetry, straight lines and the color wheel. When coloring images inspired by traditional cultures, you shouldn't be either!

Descriptions

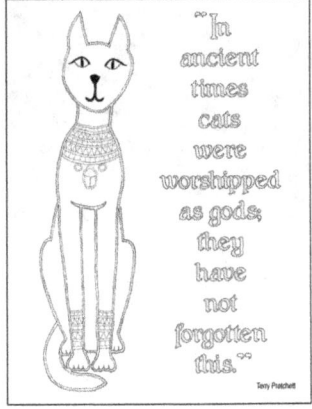

1. <u>ONCE A GOD...</u> We are all familiar with the independence, even disdain, of our feline friends. Terry Pratchet has a great quote that sums this up; I've contributed an Egyptian cat all decked out in her turquoise, red jasper, gold, green malachite, and deep blue lapis lazuli finery.

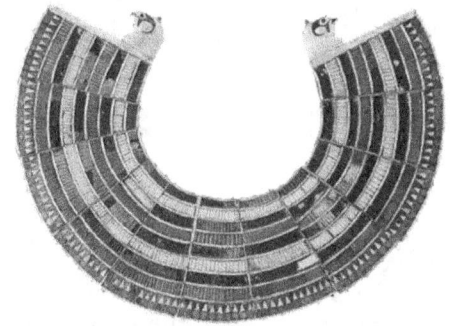 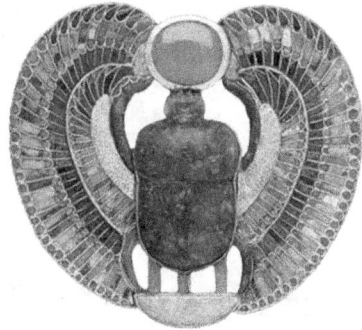

Jewelry discovered in the tomb of Tutankhamun displays the color palette of the ancient Egyptians. (see color detail on back cover)

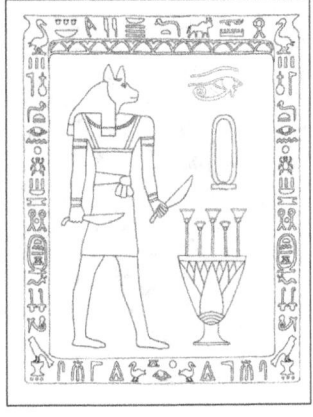

2. <u>BASTET - CAT GODDESS</u> In early Egypt the god Bast was a lioness warrior. Over time she became Bastet, a cat who protected her followers from disease and maleficent influence.

Blue Cat
by Zeny Fuentes

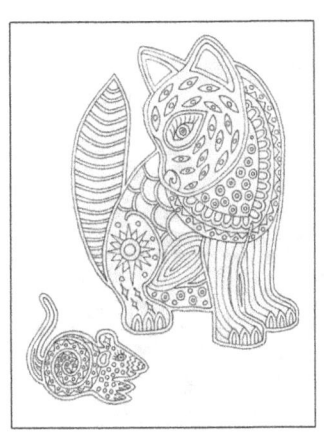

3. <u>OAXACAN CAT AND MOUSE</u> Oaxacan wood carvings from central Mexico are hand shaped and painted in a wide variety of bright colors. Whimsical and playful, this folk art style has roots that go back to the Aztecs.

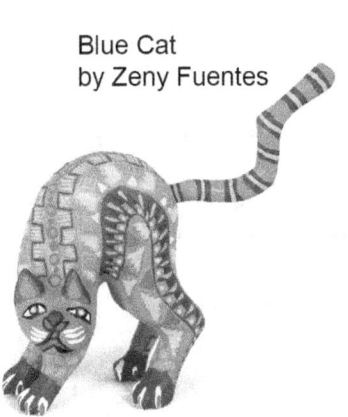

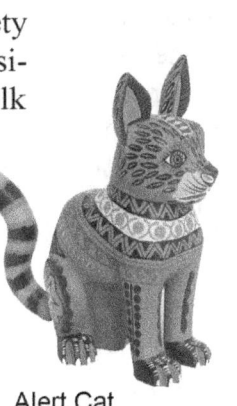

Check out SandiaFolk.com for more wonderful artful crafts from this area.

Alert Cat
by Lauro Ramirez

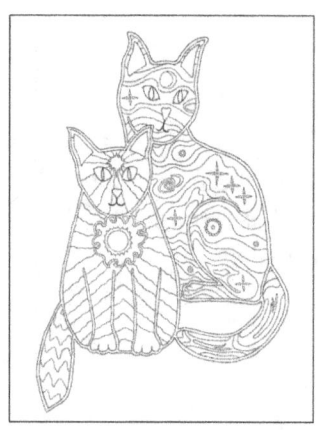

4. NIGHT & DAY CATS A friend described her cats as being as different as night and day. I pictured a sun-worshipping Aztec cat accompanied by her nocturnal friend whose glorious celestial patterns come from cosmic photographs shot by the Hubble Telescope.

Images taken by the Hubble Telescope can be found at hubblesite.org/images/gallery.

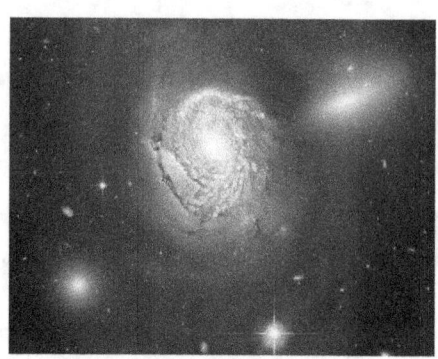

Spiral Galaxy NGC 4911
in the Coma Cluster

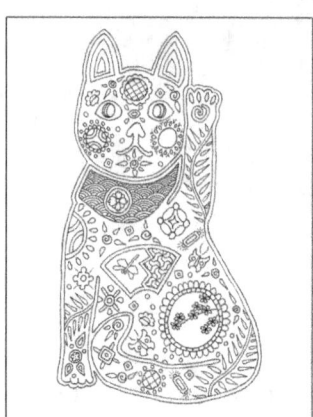

5. BECKONING CAT Maneki-neko is the beckoning cat popular in Japan. It brings good luck and great fortune.

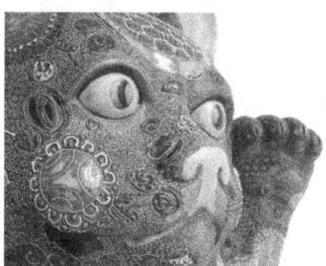

This cat is decorated in a style called moriage - raised slip lines or beads that provide texture to ceramics. (My inspiration was featured on etsy for a mere $9,999.)

Detail of etsy
beckoning cat

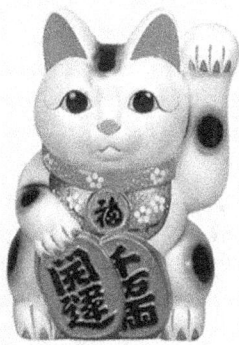

Modern version
of beckoning cat

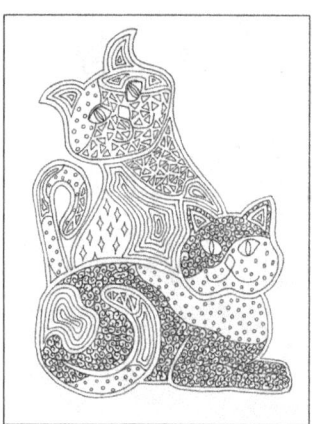

6. CALICO COUPLE   For many years I was unable to draw cats, they just never seemed right, until two calico cats came to me with enough individual personality and style to get me over the block. Calico cats are considered lucky. Fishermen in Japan kept a calico cat shipboard for protection from gales and ghosts.

Clay kitty
decoupaged
with calico fabric

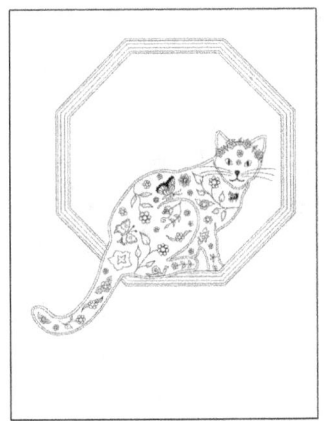

7. <u>LAURIE'S CAT</u> Cat portrait drawn for a friend. Perched on the window-sill, she is surveying her domain, while enjoying the sun, the beauty, and the bounty of nature. I found two quotes that perfectly express this scene for me:

"The ideal of calm exists in a sitting cat." – Jules Reynard;

and, paradoxically,

"It always gives me a shiver when I see a cat seeing what I can't see."
– Eleanor Farjeon

A classic Japanese *Ukiyo-e* woodblock that also depicts a cat at the window in quiet contemplation. Notice the stubby tail in both the woodblock and paper dolls. Often cats in Asia have shortened tails.

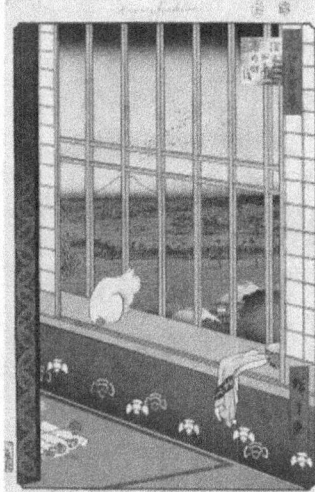

8. <u>JAPANESE PAPER DOLLS</u>
Japan has a long tradition of including cats in both esteemed artwork and popular culture.

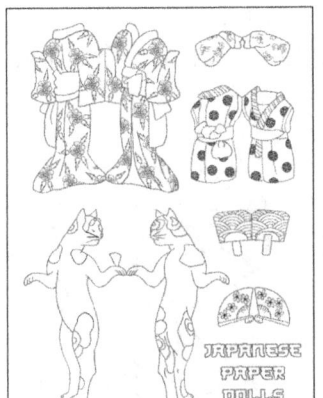

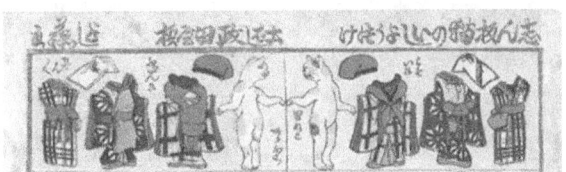

Detail from the website tofugu.com; an informative look at cats in Japanese art and culture.

Utagawa Hiroshige No. 101 from One Hundred Famous Views of Edo

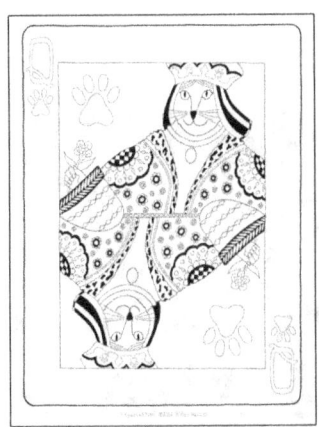

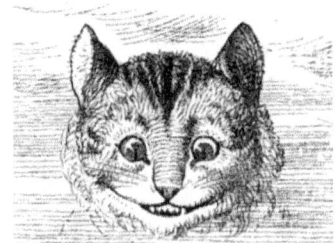

9. <u>QUEEN OF PAWS</u> I love the story and imagery in *Alice in Wonderland* and drew Queen of Paws as a fusion of the Queen of Hearts (in a less authoritarian frame of mind) and the Cheshire Cat.

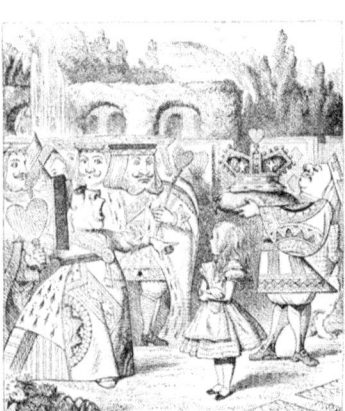

John Tenniel created the first illustrations (after Lewis Carrol) for *Alice in Wonderland.*

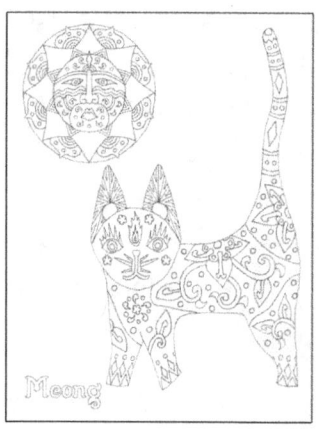

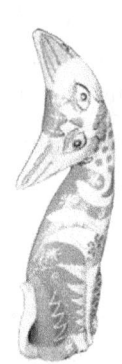

10. <u>MEONG</u> Balinesians do not generally have as great a fondness for cats as do folks in the United States. However Balinese artisans carve whimsical cats vividly painted with traditional designs familiar from batik fabric. Meong is the Indonesian word for meow.

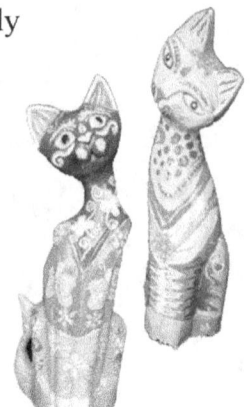

I found these colorful kitties on Balique.com

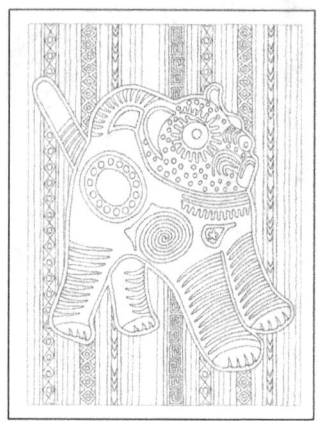

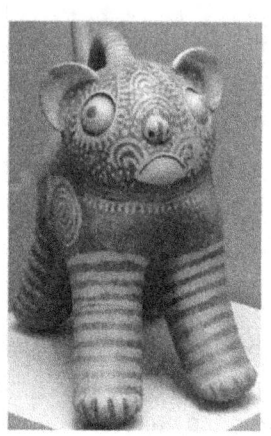

American Museum
of Natural History
Photo: Kevin Wiley

11. <u>GRUMPY CAT</u> This grumpy cat was looted by grave robbers in northern Peru and found its way into the collection of the American Museum of Natural History. It is a Pre-Colombian ceramic bottle, a hole at the end of the tail to permit drinking.

The people who created this cat would have a high regard for cats because by killing mice and rats, they protected harvests. In the background are Peruvian weaving patterns.

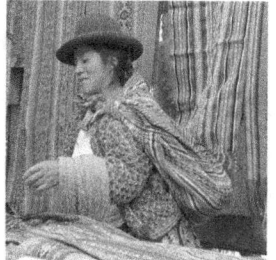

From the website of
Best of Peru Travel

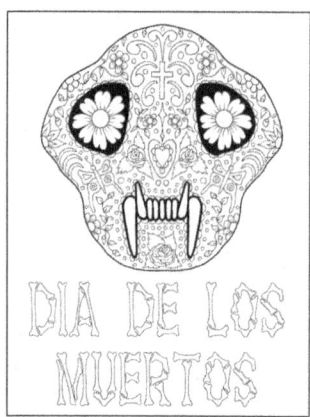

12. <u>DIA DE LOS MUERTOS</u> Sugar skulls are a much appreciated gift for both the living and the dead on the Day of the Dead. Dia de los Muertos is celebrated in Mexico as a time to remember and pray for family and friends who died recently. My sugar skull is feline rather than the traditional human skull.

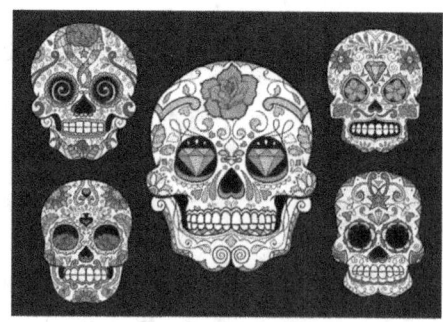

Skulls compliments of InkyDeals.com

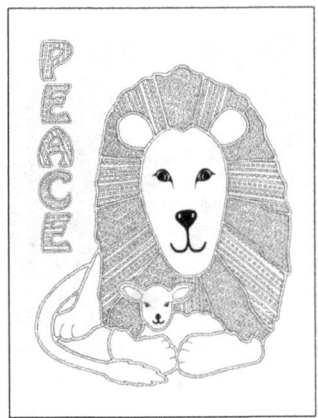

13. <u>PEACE LION</u> Imagine my surprise when I was researching a description for the iconic "Lion and Lamb" and found that in the biblical quote they do not even appear together! My lion has a mane filled

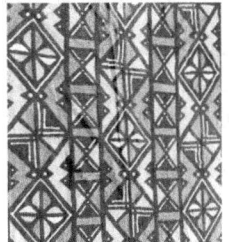

with mudcloth designs from Mali. To make mudcloth, men first weave the cloth, then women paint the designs, each of which is rich in meaning.

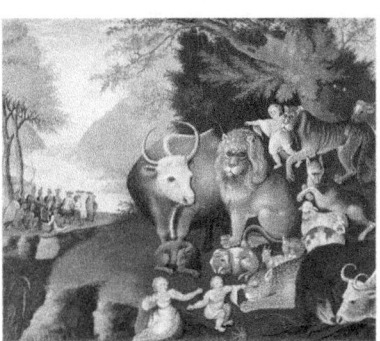

One of my favorite paintings: The Peaceable Kingdom (1826) Edward Hicks

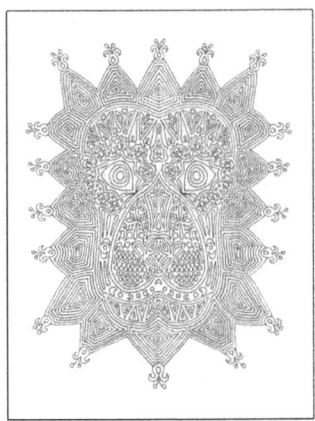

14. <u>PSYCHEDELIC LION</u> Louis Wain was a popular illustrator in Victorian England who often portrayed cats in human activities. He was committed numerous times to various institutions, where he kept drawing cats - they became increasingly bizarre and unfriendly. I drew a lion in a style I'd call "early schizophrenic," but, alas, I couldn't pull it off and my lion looks pretty friendly. Perhaps we should just call it psychedelic?

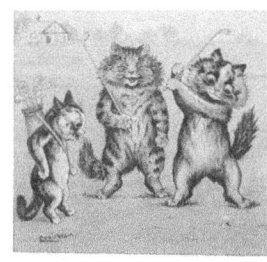

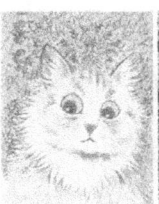 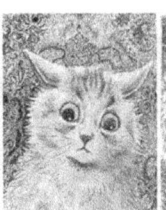 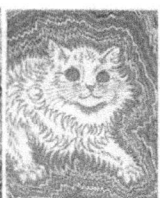 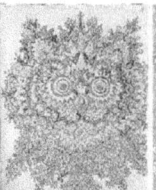 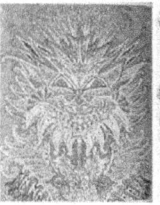 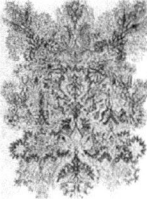

Louis Wain's cats, drawn while institutionalized.

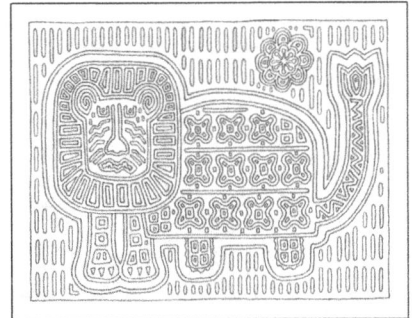

15. <u>MOLA LION</u> While living in Panama I came to love molas, cloth panels sewn and worn by Kuna women. Molas are layered fabric; often the top layer is a deep red or orange, the bottom black, and the middle layer whatever the artist feels like. The material used for appliqué and placed under the cut-outs are the widest variety of colors you can imagine, arranged in sections to utilize scrap material. The lion here is a Kuna woman's interpretation of a lion that originated in 60's children's fabric.

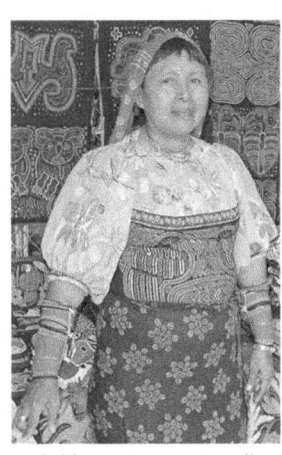

A Kuna woman sells her molas.

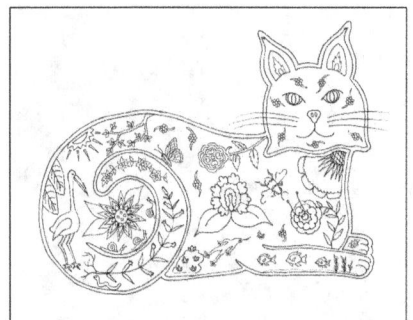

16. CAT IMAGINATION

I tried to fill this chintz cat with all of the things I imagined her imagining. While Edgar Allen Poe wished he "could write as mysterious as a cat," I wished to draw her mystery. Again, my tone is a bit lighter!

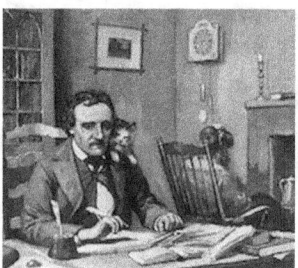

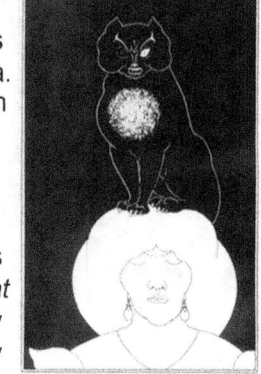

Edgar Allan Poe and his tortoiseshell cat, Catterina. Drawn by Chas. Sheldon

Illustration for Poe's *The Black Cat* by Aubrey Beardsley

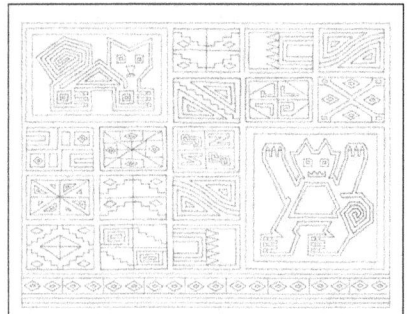

17. INCAN CATS

Incan people used the wool of llamas and alpacas to weave tunics with beautiful geometric designs.

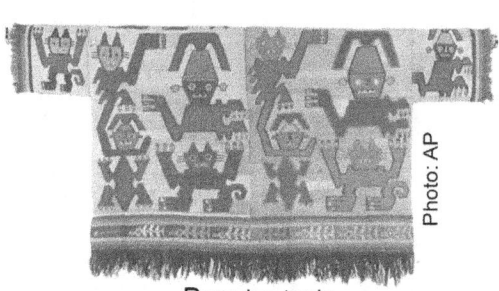

Photo: AP

Peruvian tunic
in The Andean Tunic: 400 BCE-1800 CE
exhibit at The Metropolitan Museum of Art.

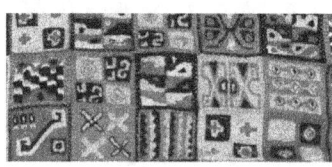

Inca royal tunic weaving detail.

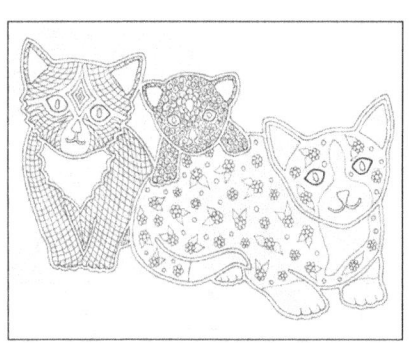

18. THREE KITTENS

Ogden Nash has a well known ditty: *"The trouble with a kitten is that eventually it becomes a cat."* The other trouble, for me anyway, was figuring out how to draw a kitten versus a cat when I was commissioned to draw a few. It took some doing... Ogden Nash also wrote some of the screenplay for the Wizard of Oz movie.

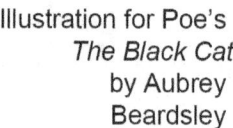

The Cowardly Lion from
The Wonderful Wizard of Oz,
drawn by William Wallace Denslow

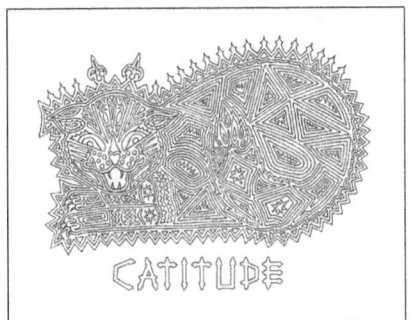

19. <u>CATITUDE</u> anybody with a cat in their life has experienced it!

"They're cute and furry and cuddly, but we need to remember when we have cats as pets, we are inviting little predators into our house, Cats can be fantastic, sweet companions — until they turn on you."
Max Wachtel

"Those who'll play with cats must expect to be scratched."
Miguel deCervantes
author of *Don Quixote.*

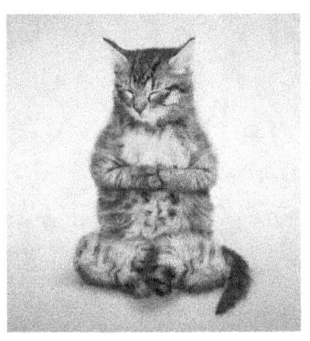

Etching by
Félix Bracquemond
captures the "warning look"
given just before a scratch.

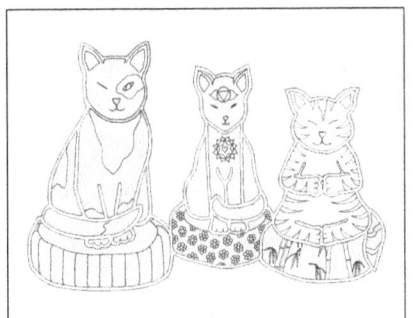

20. <u>MEDITATING CATS</u> Another wonderful cat quote comes from Eckhart Tolle, *"I have lived with several Zen masters – all of them cats."* Here are a few cats on their zafu pillows proving his point.

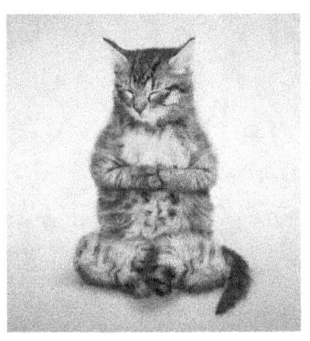

This is Miles,
in the lotus pose in a
Yoga Catz calendar.

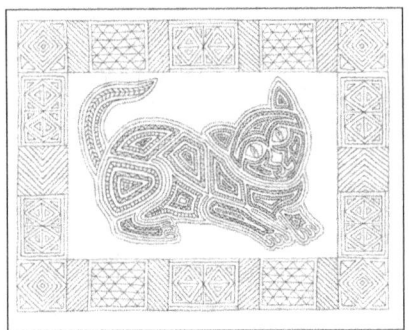

21. <u>GUATEMALAN GATO</u> This playful kitty is surrounded by and filled with the wonderful patterns found in Guatemalan backstrap weaving. The multicolored belt I wore almost every day in high school was similar to that pictured below.

Edward Leers' tabby cat Foss looks quite playful.

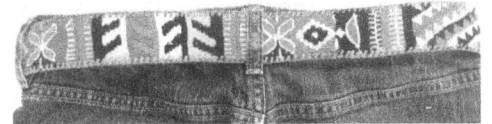

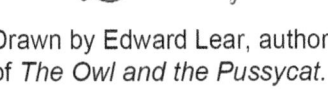

Drawn by Edward Lear, author
of *The Owl and the Pussycat.*

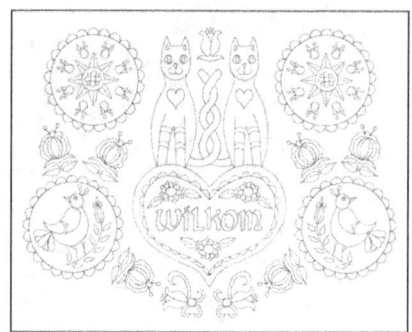

22. <u>HEX SIGNS</u> In a book entitled Hex Signs, the author's well regarded take was that, *"the meanings we find in the hex signs are ethnic identity, ethnic pride, and the pure joy of colorful decoration."*

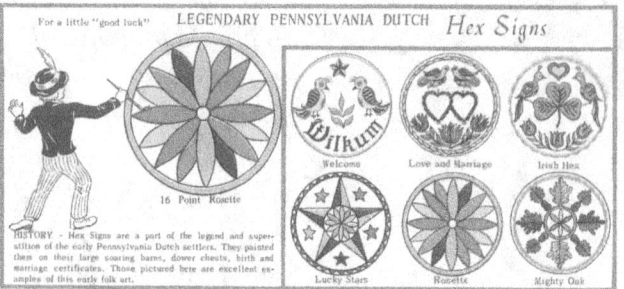

A vintage hex postcard found on postcardy.com.

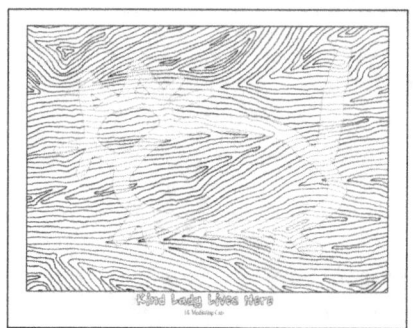

23. <u>A KIND LADY LIVES HERE</u> This cat was a message, often carved into fenceposts at the house of a woman who would share food with a hobo. Hobos traveled America in the late 1800's, through the Great Depression, into the present. A harsh lifestyle was made easier by communicating helpful information to fellow travelors via hobo signs and symbols.

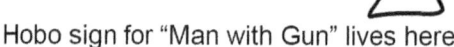

Hobo sign for "Man with Gun" lives here

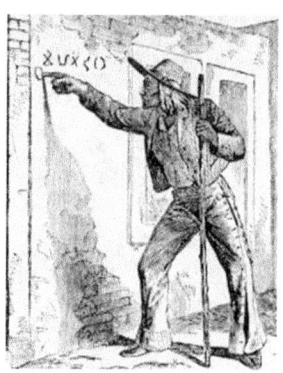

By Col. Albert S. Evans, found on wikimedia.

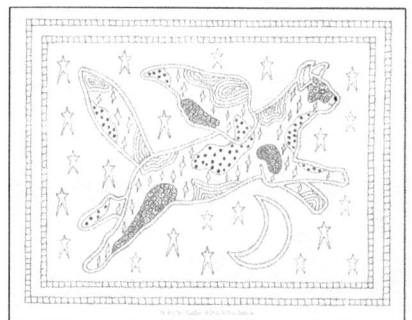

24. <u>BYE BYE PATCHES</u> Our cat, Patches, was with us for 18 years. She was a rescue kitten – my children found her in the woods after a horrible night of thunderstorms. As they were begging to keep her, she rested her head on my foot – how could I resist! When we had to put her to sleep, the vet suggested I'd feel better if I wrote her a eulogy. Instead, I drew it.

"Animals have a much better attitude to life and death than we do. They know when their time has come. We are the ones that suffer when they pass, but it's a healing kind of grief that enables us to deal with other griefs that are not so easy to grab hold of."

Emmylou Harris

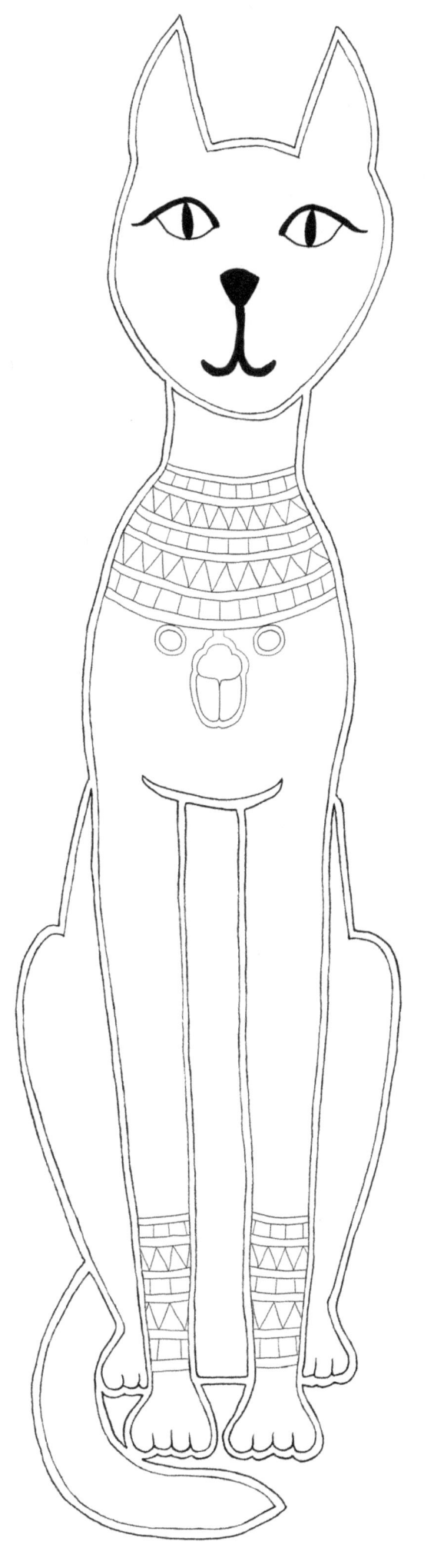

"In ancient times cats were worshipped as gods; they have not forgotten this."

Terry Pratchett

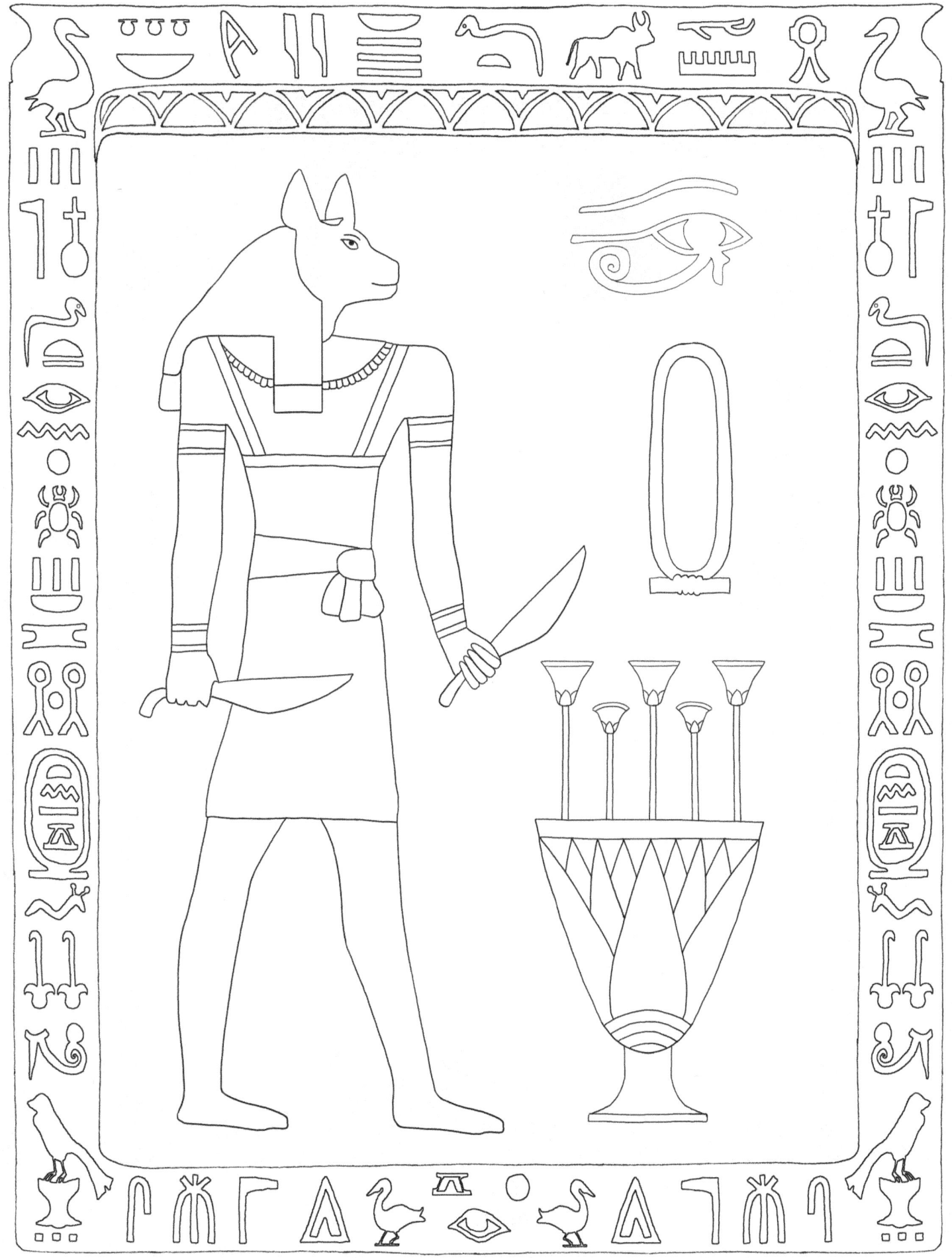

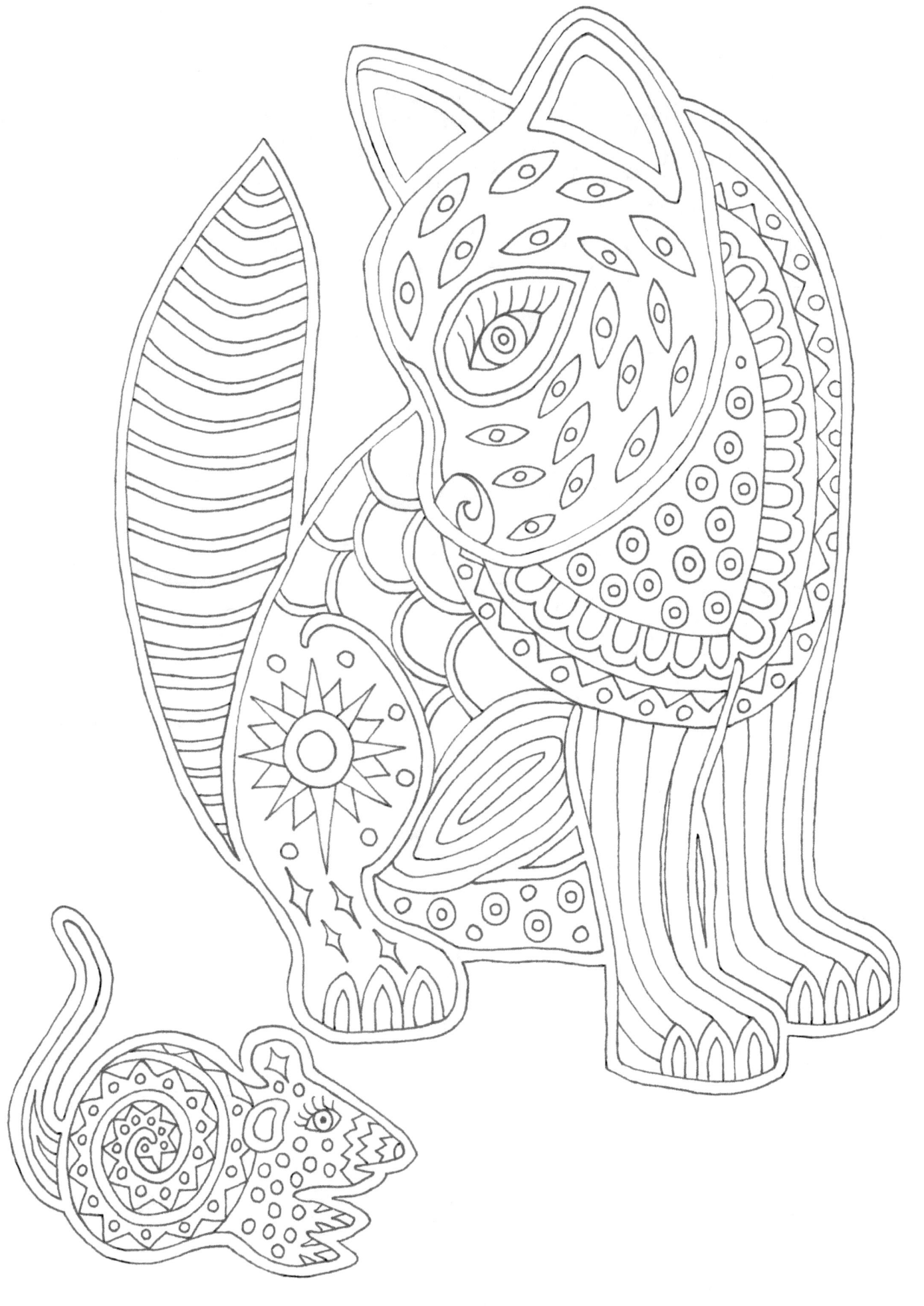

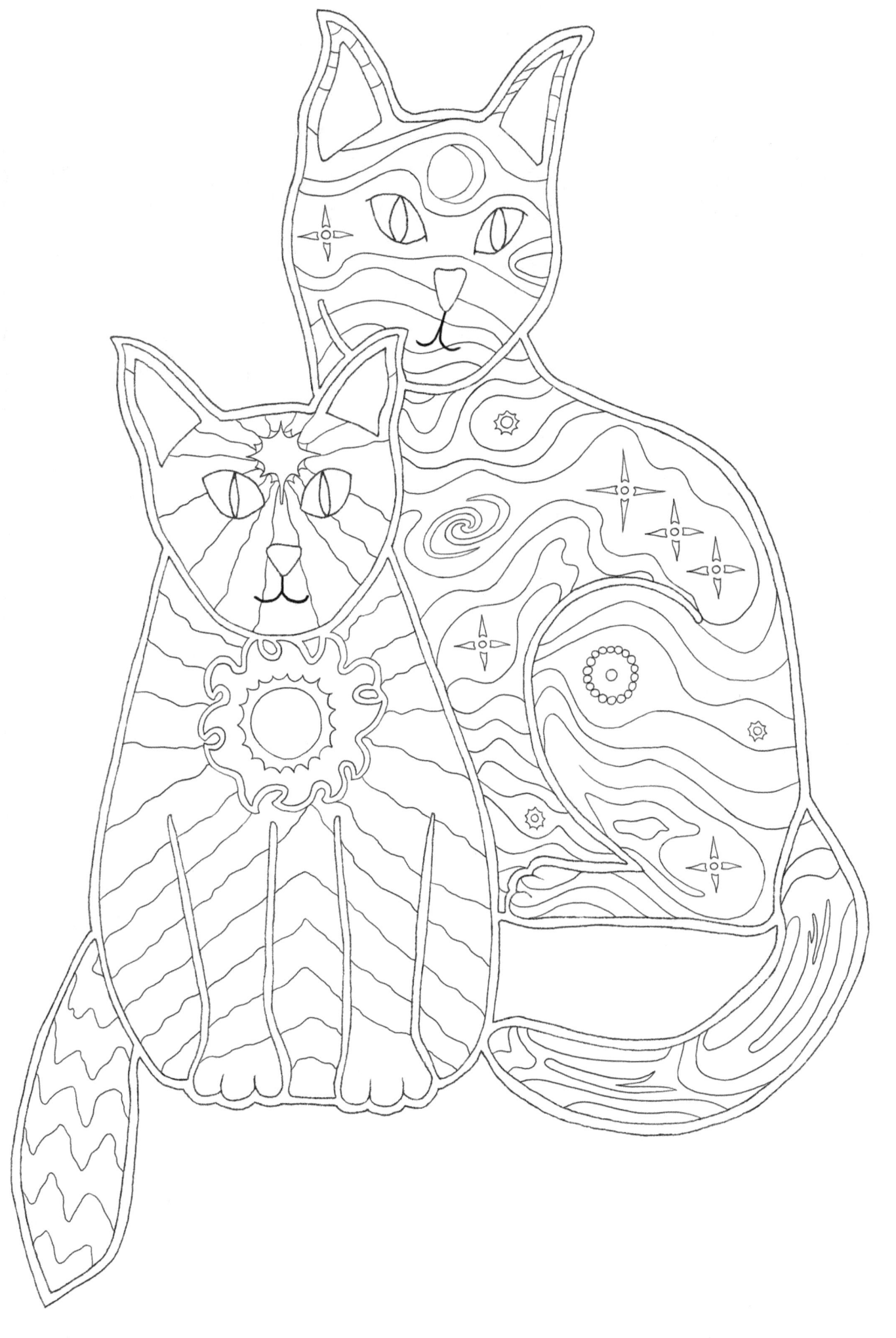

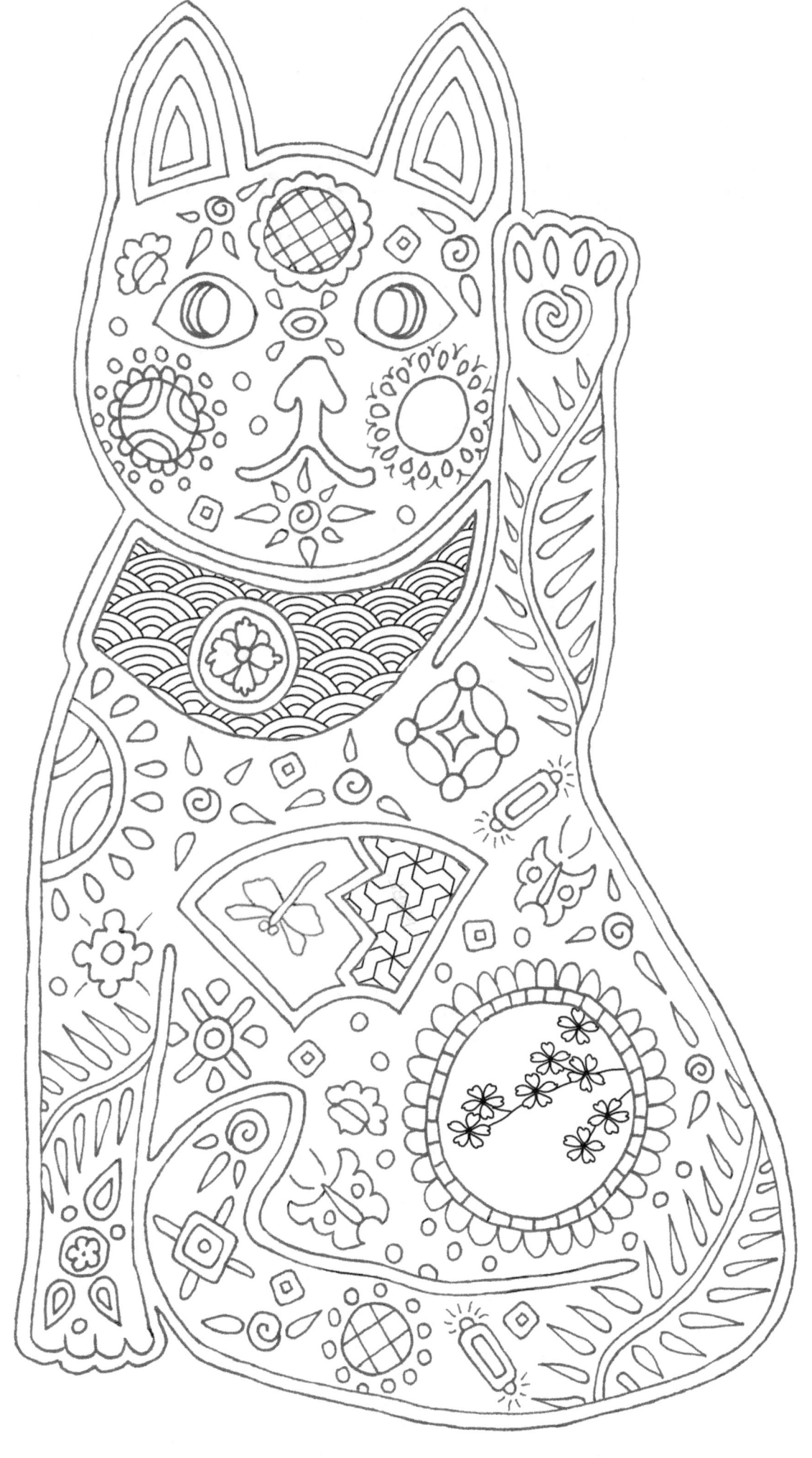

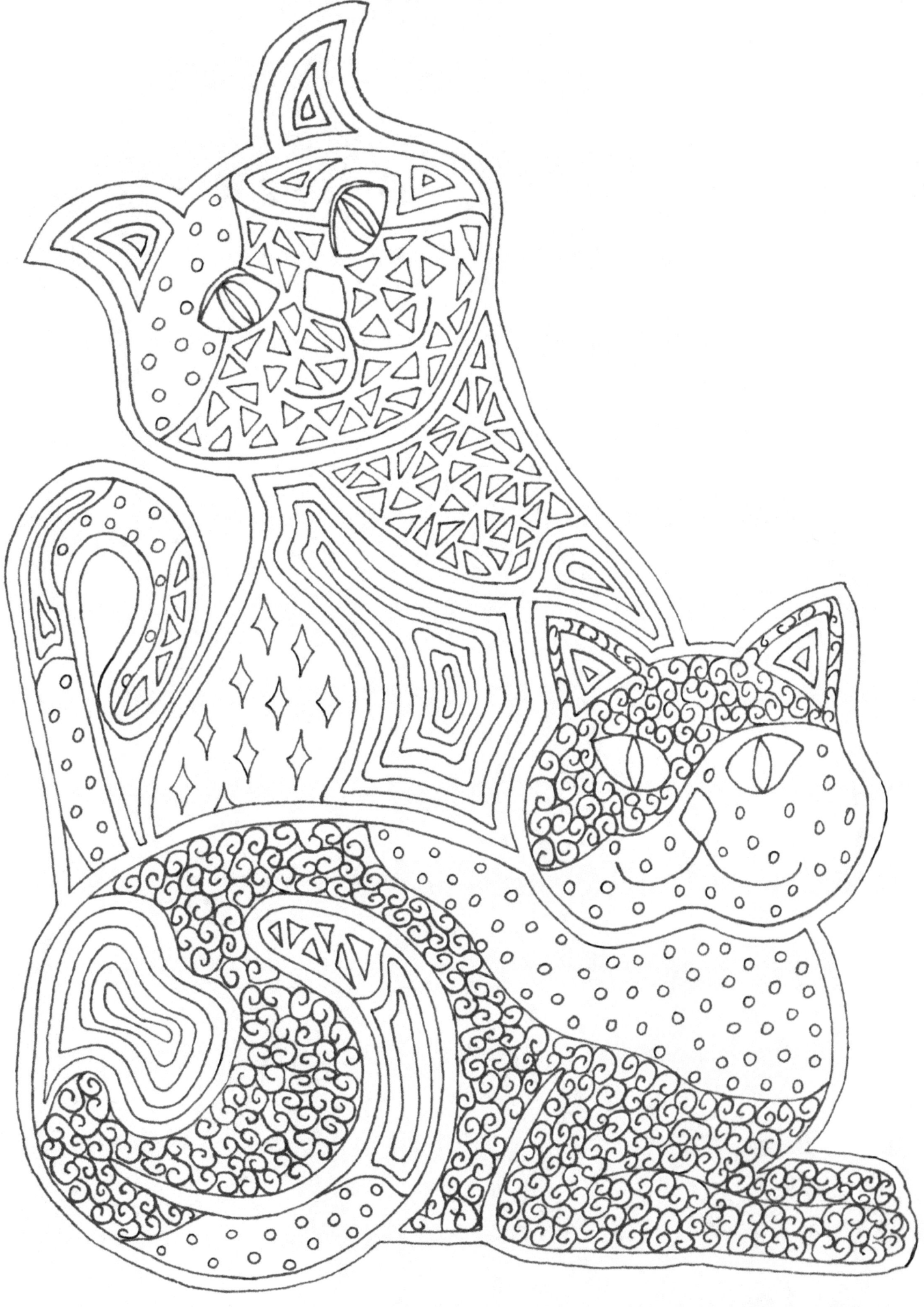

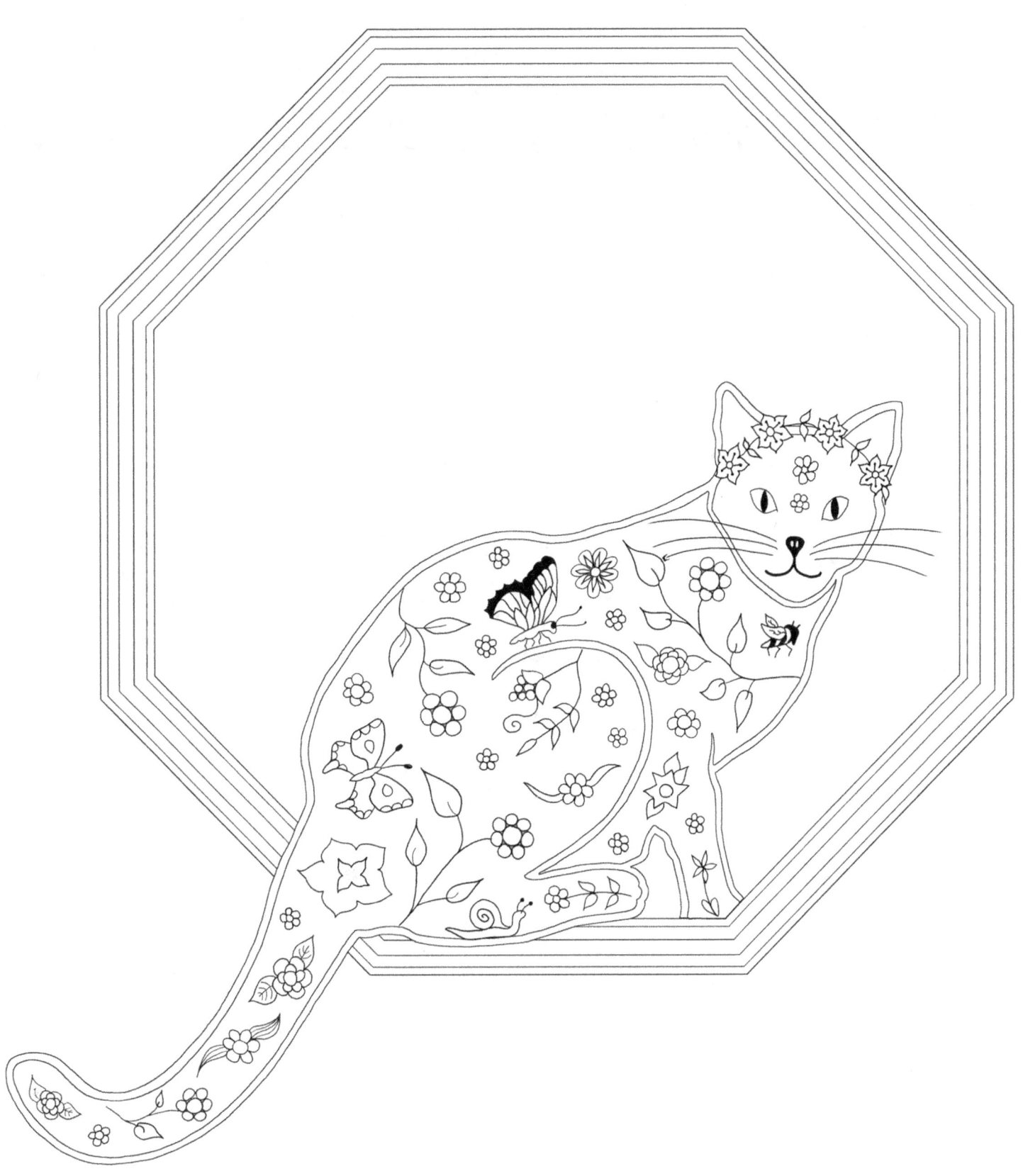

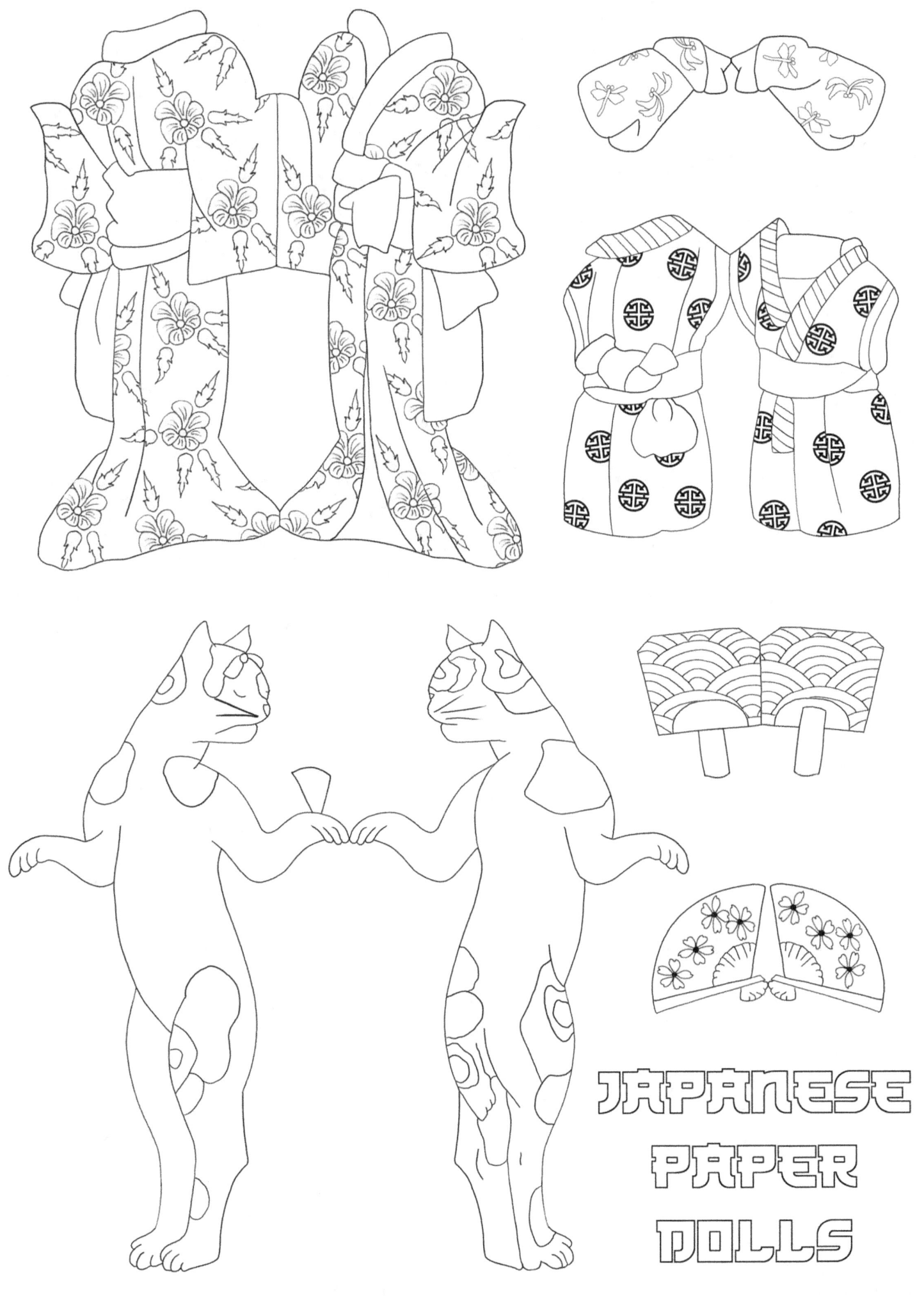

JAPANESE
PAPER
DOLLS

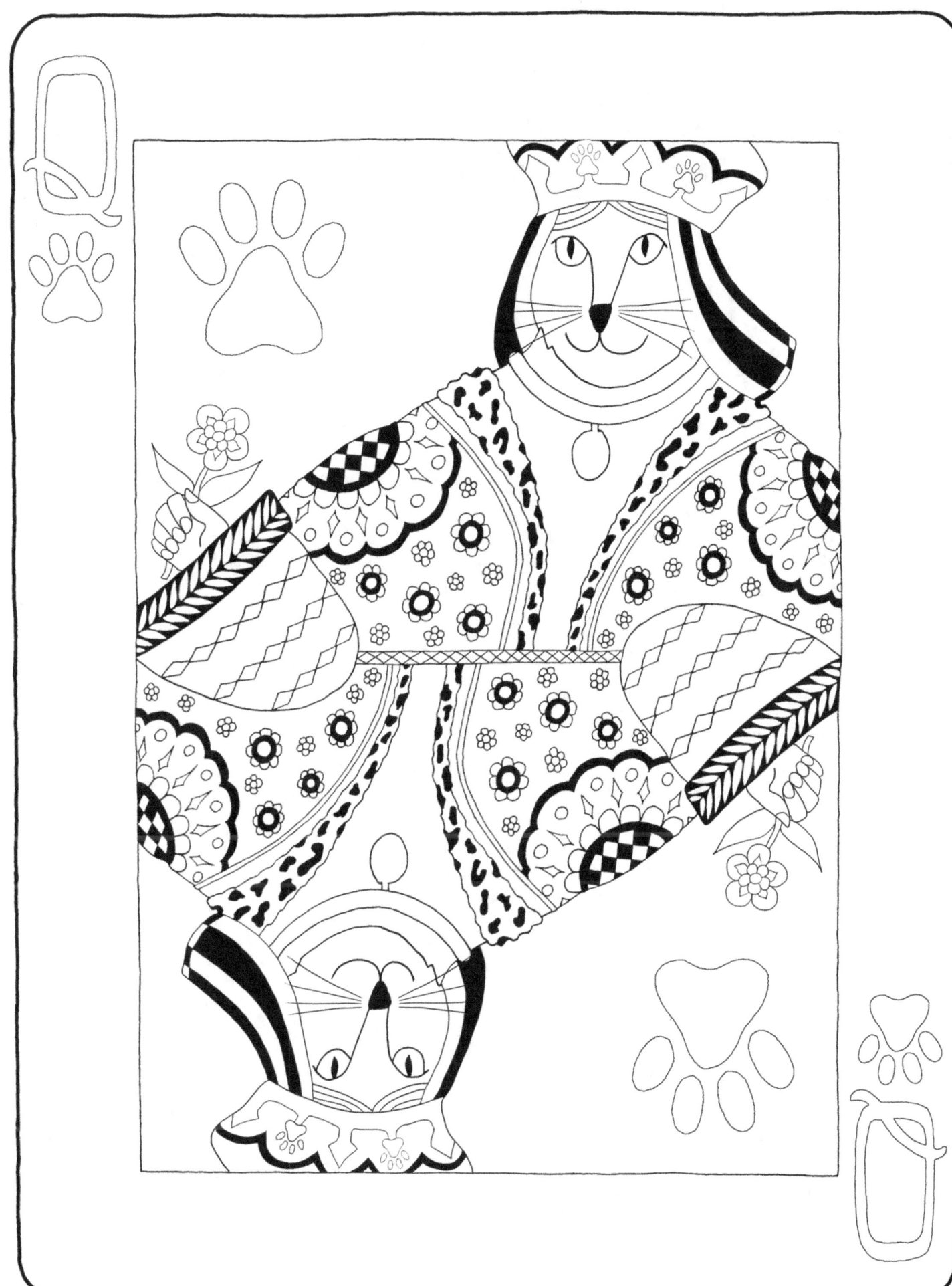

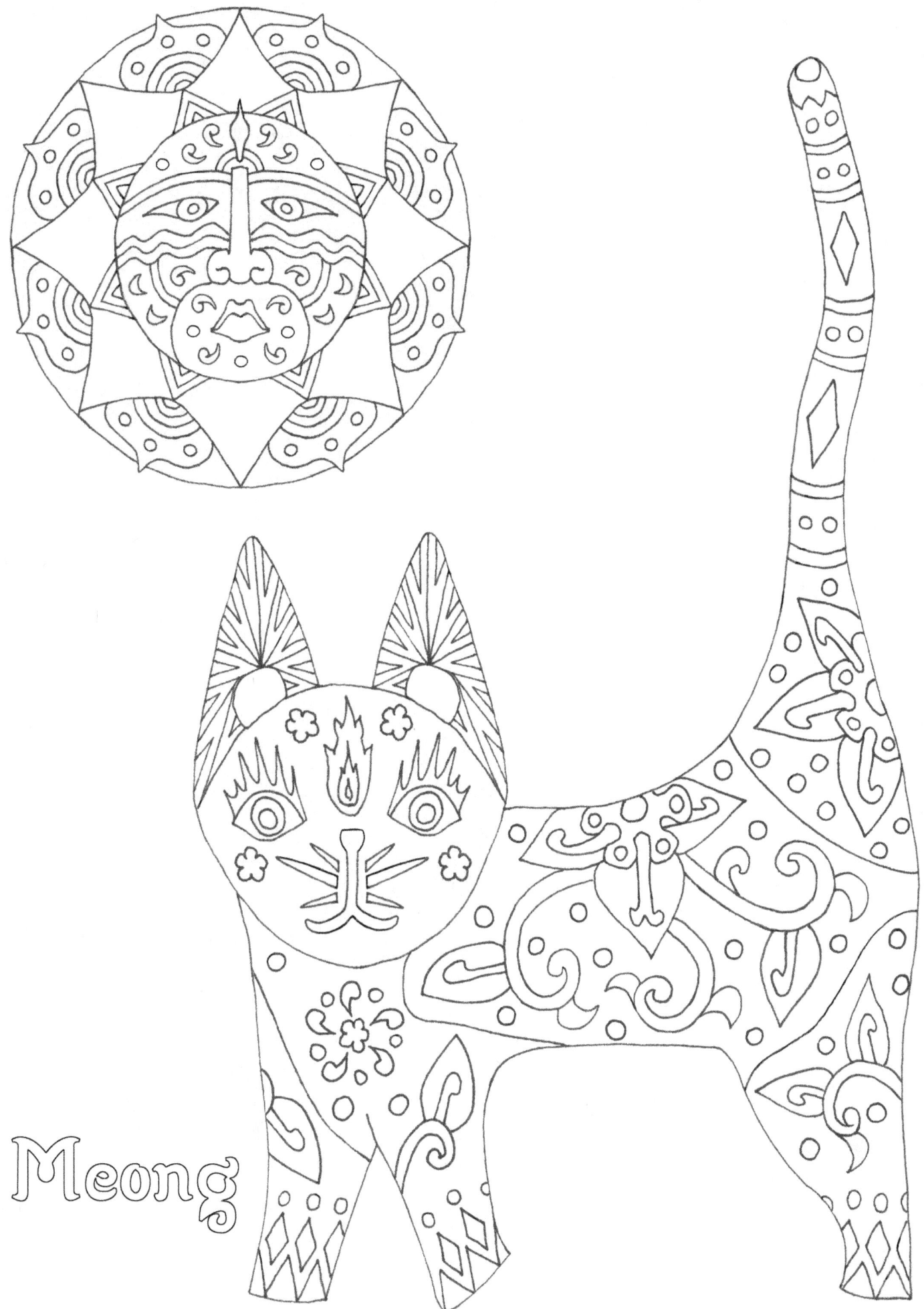

Meong

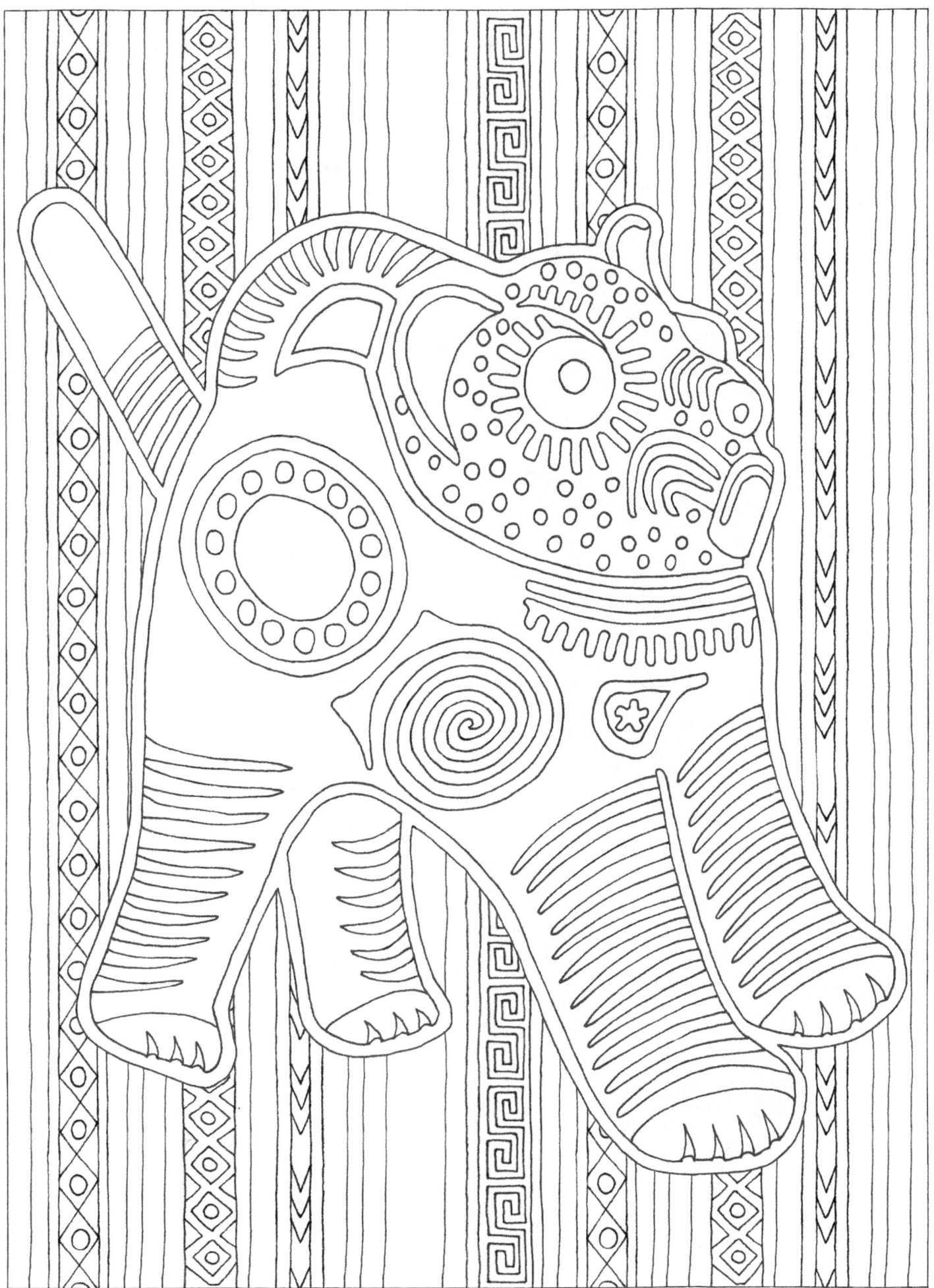

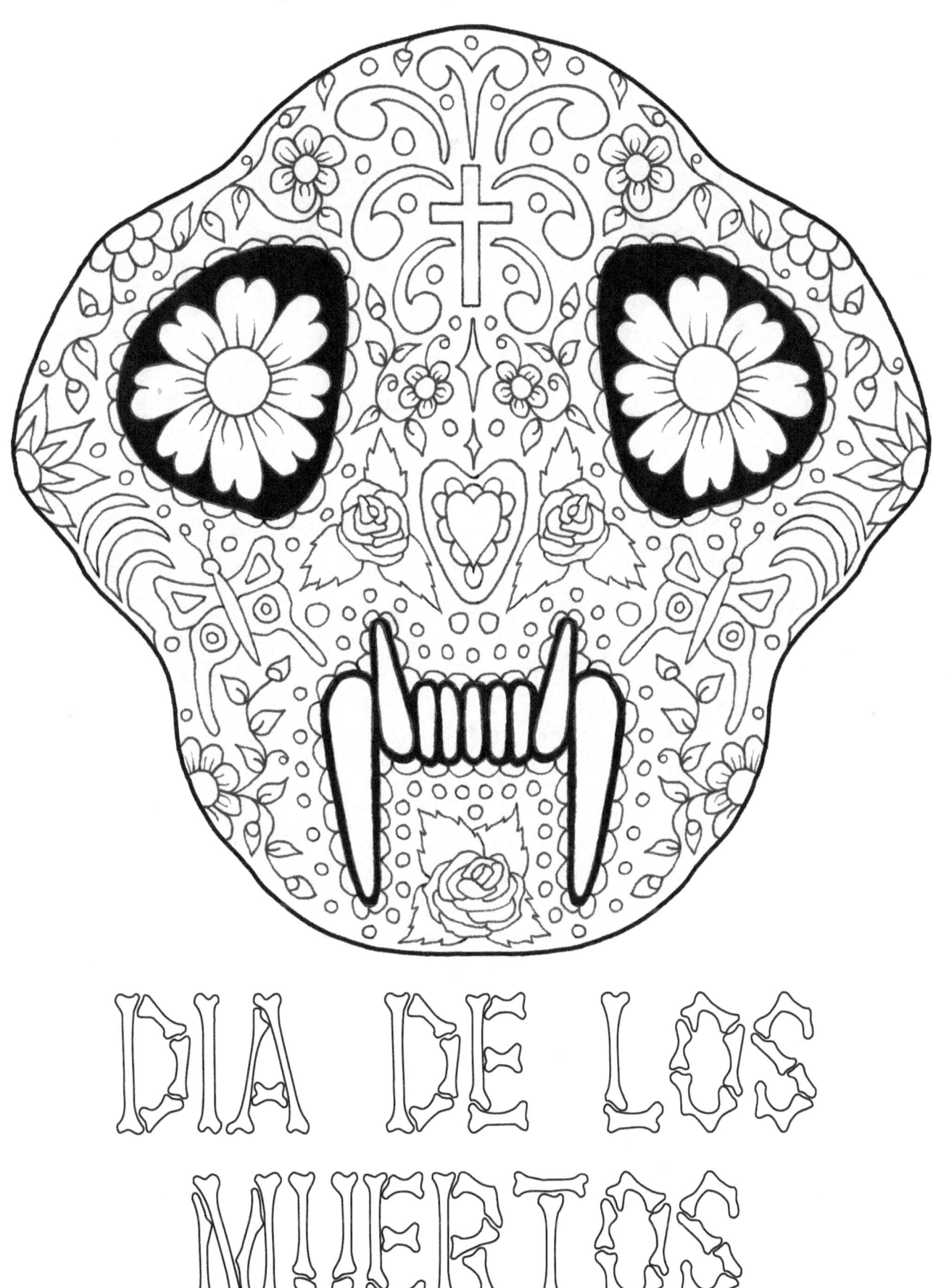

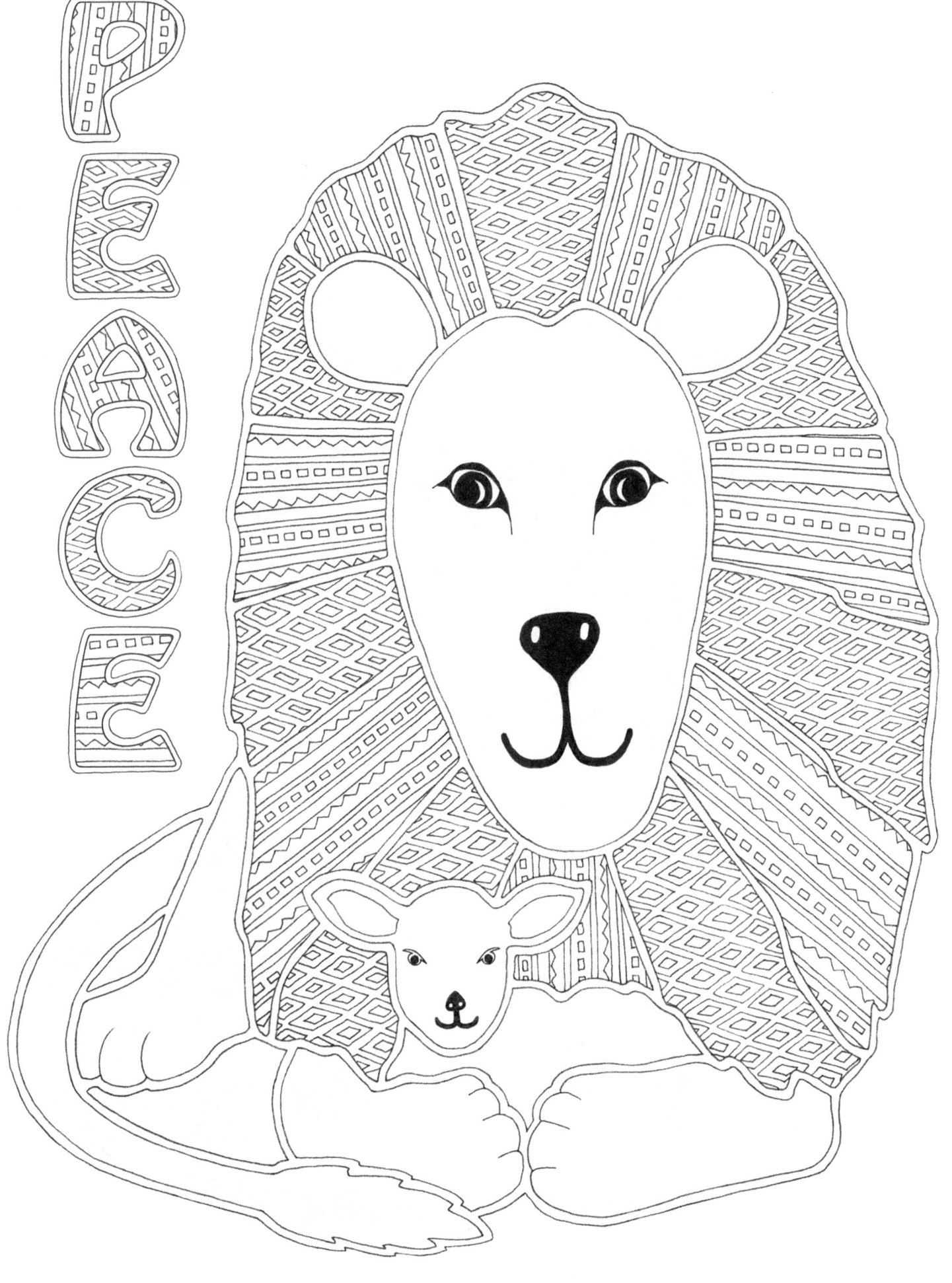

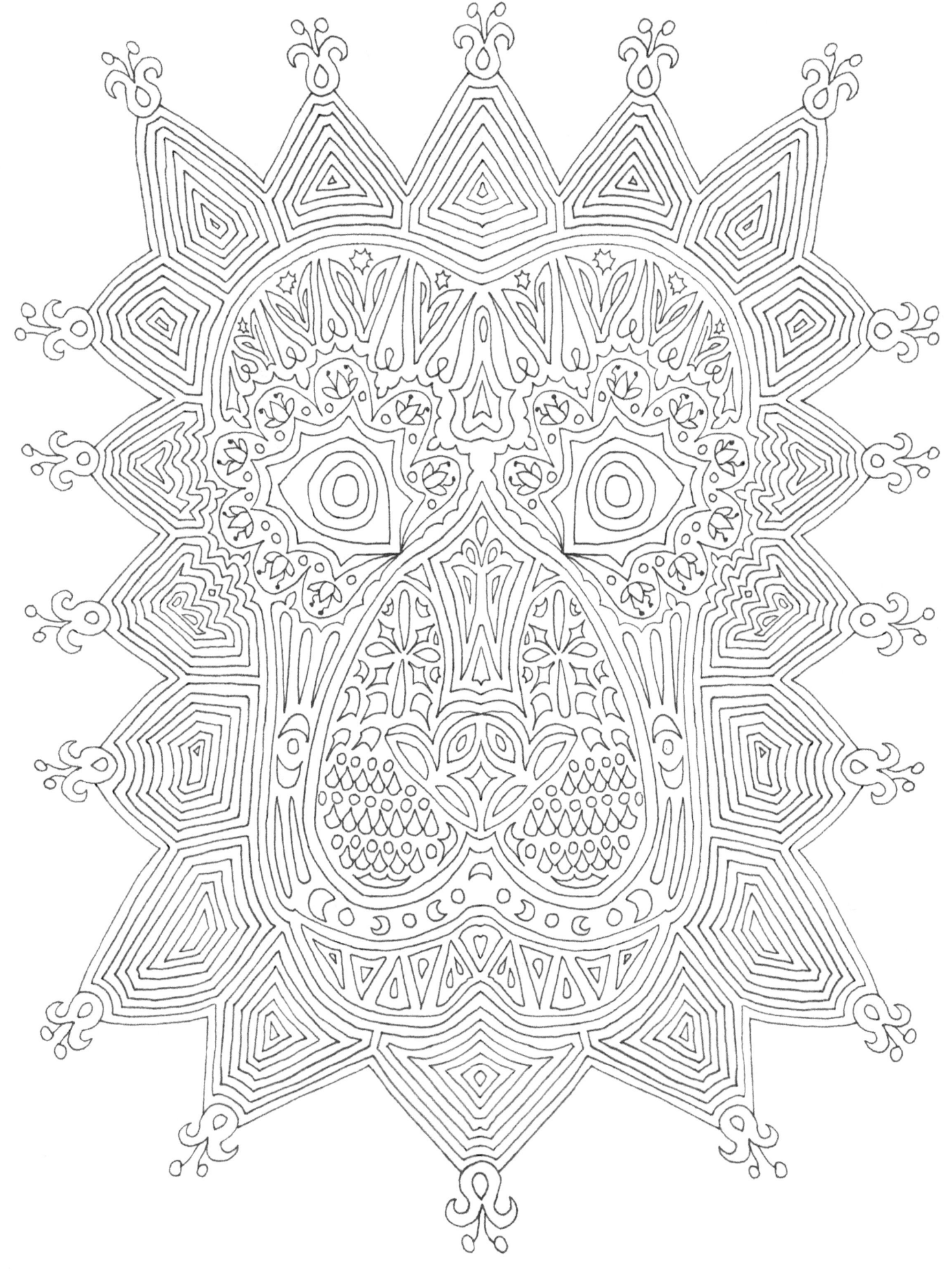

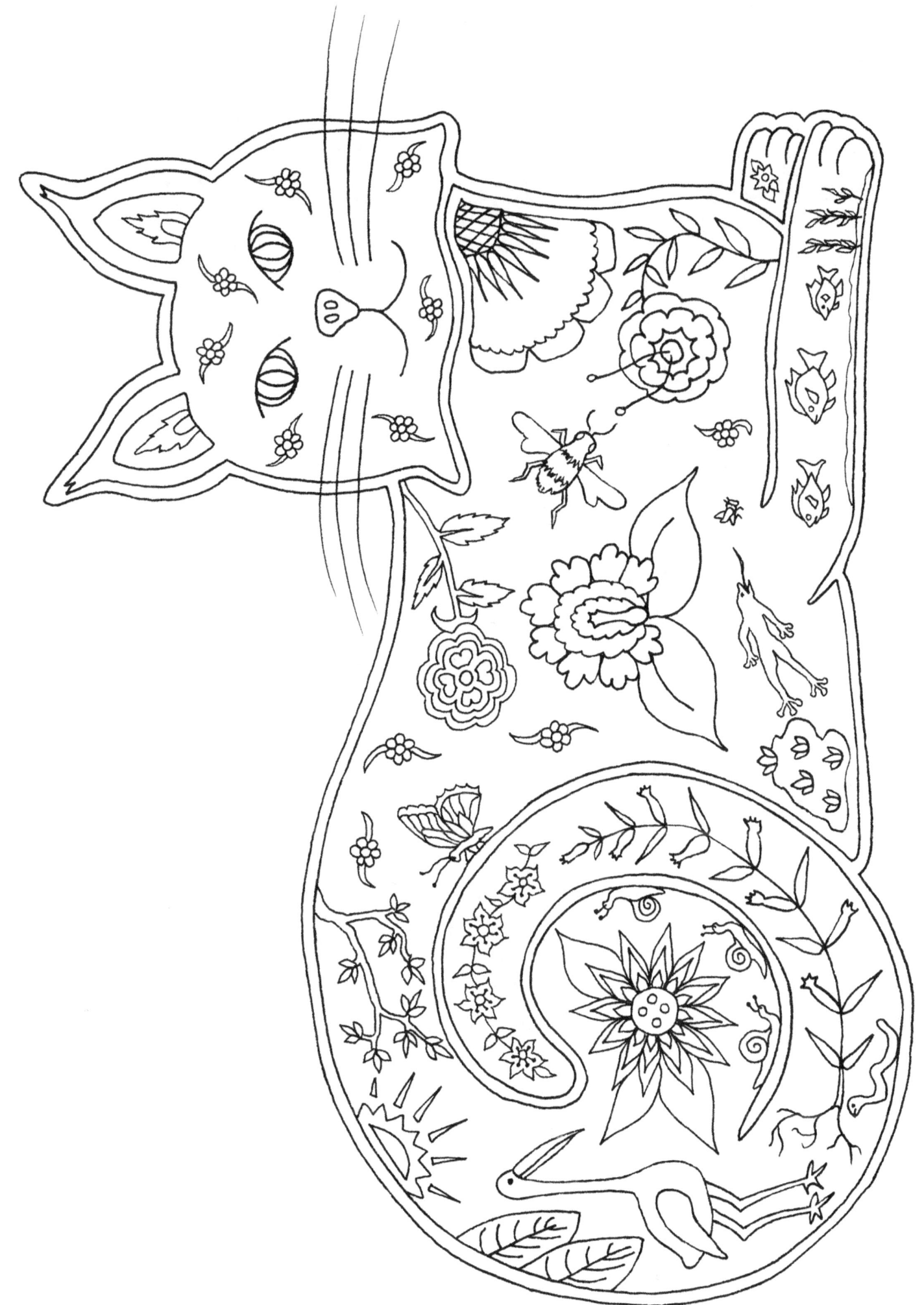

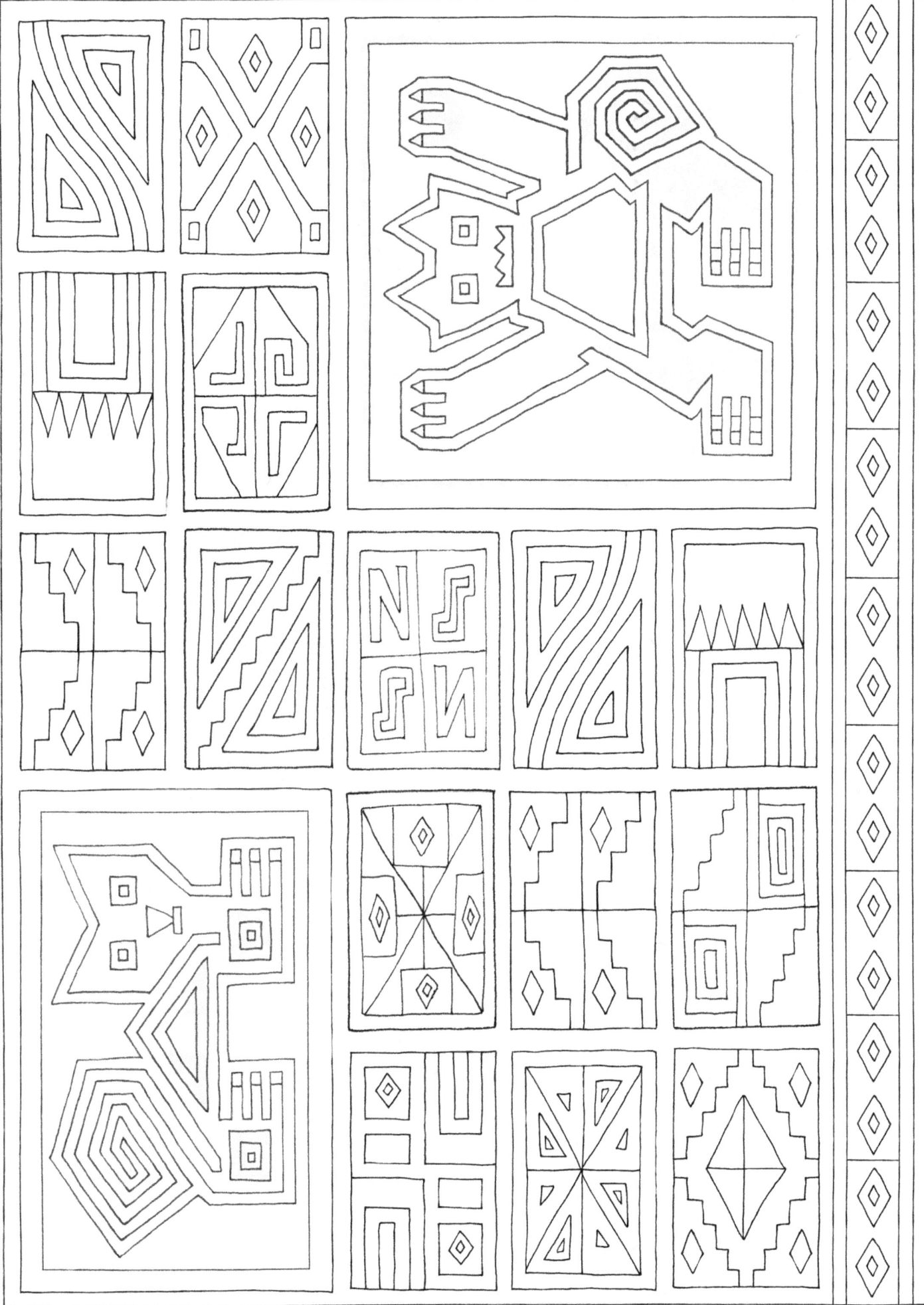

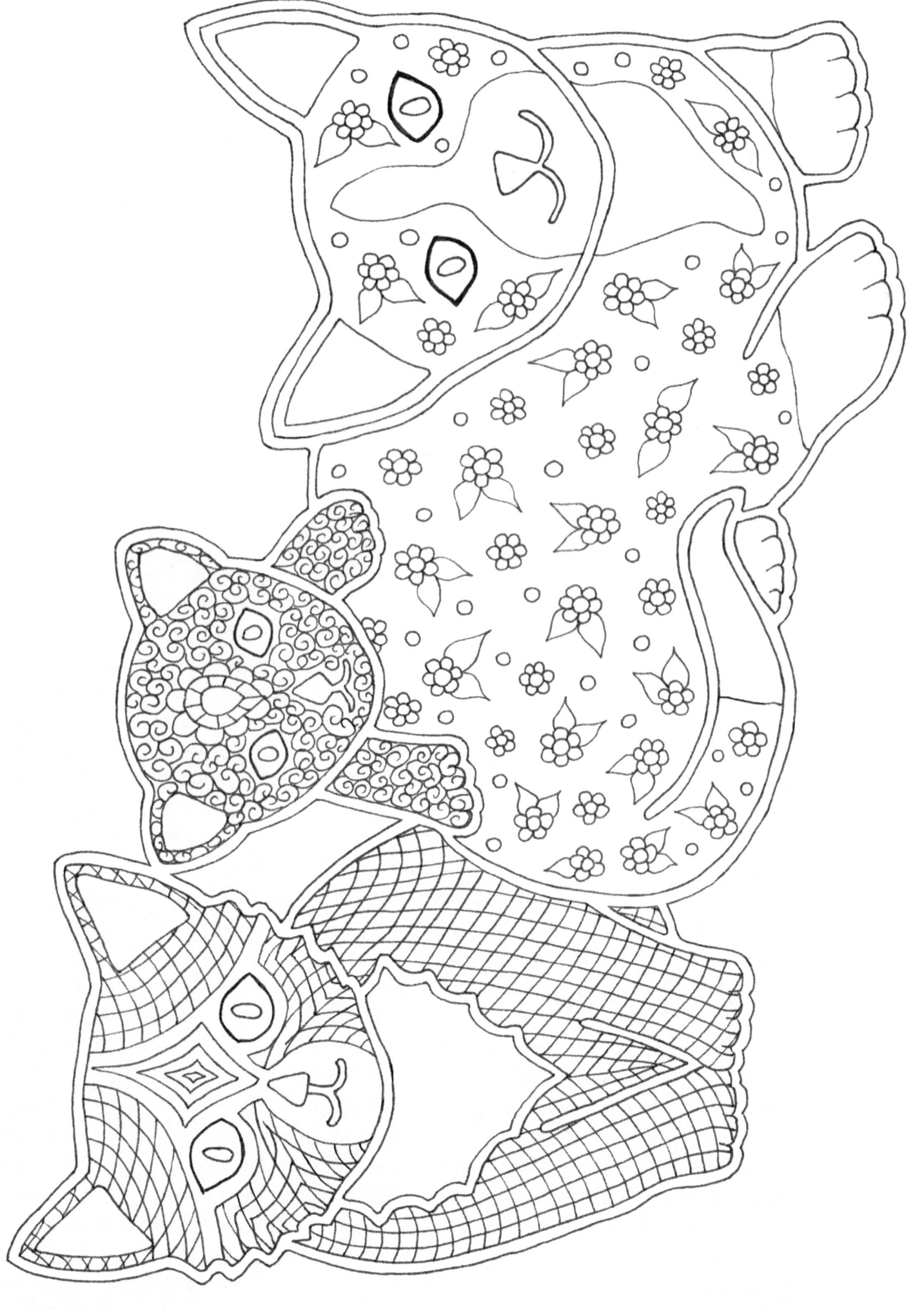

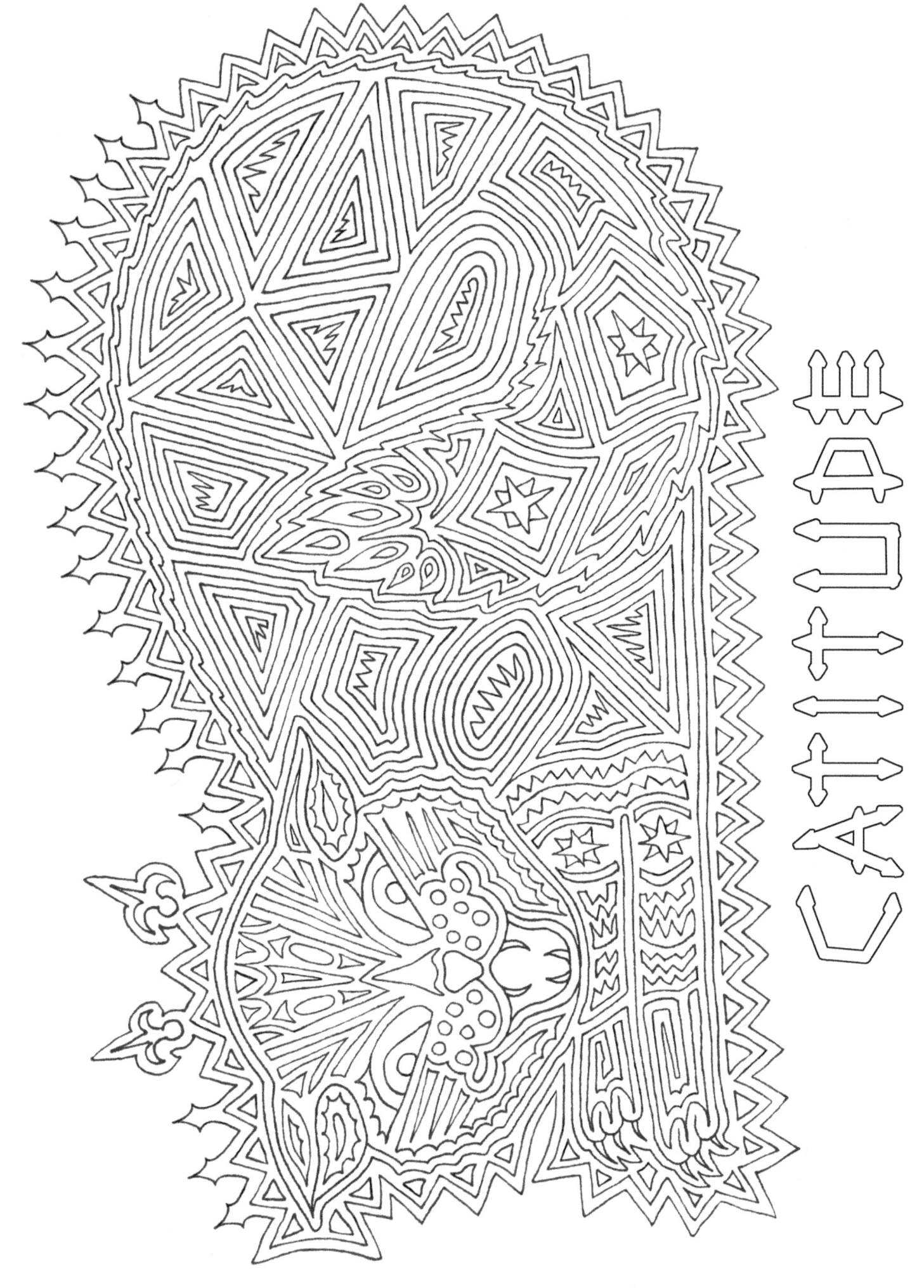

CATITUDE

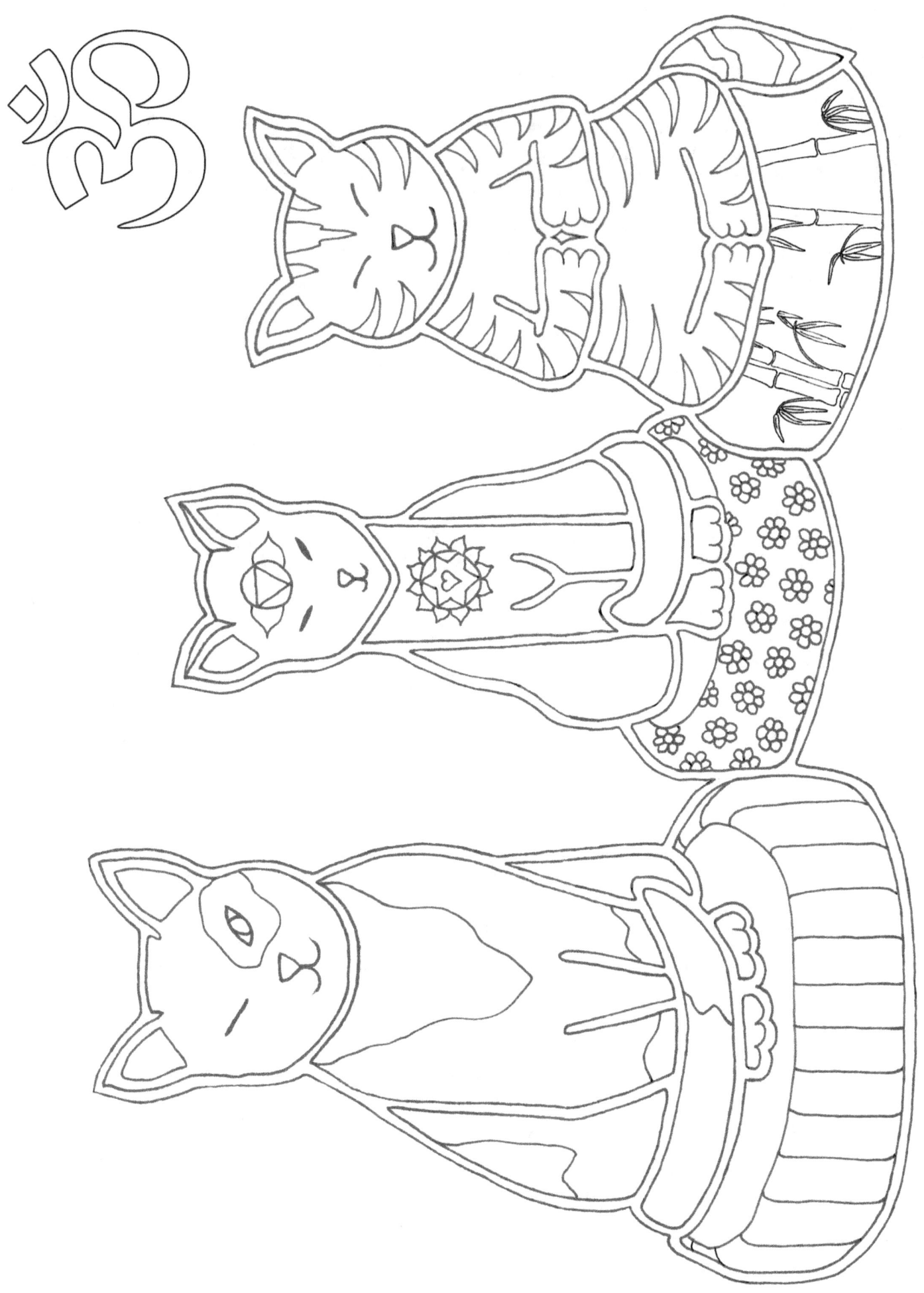

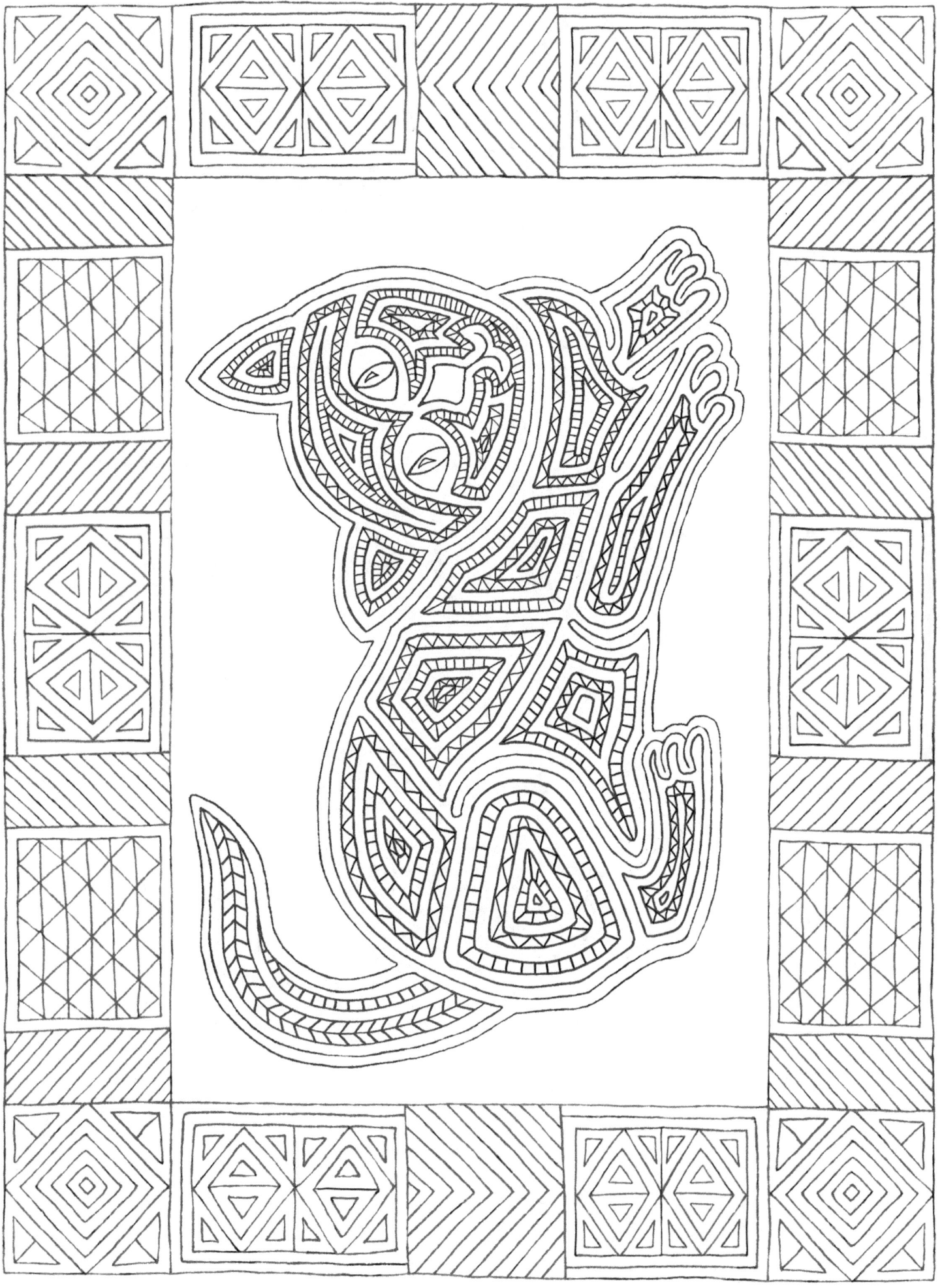

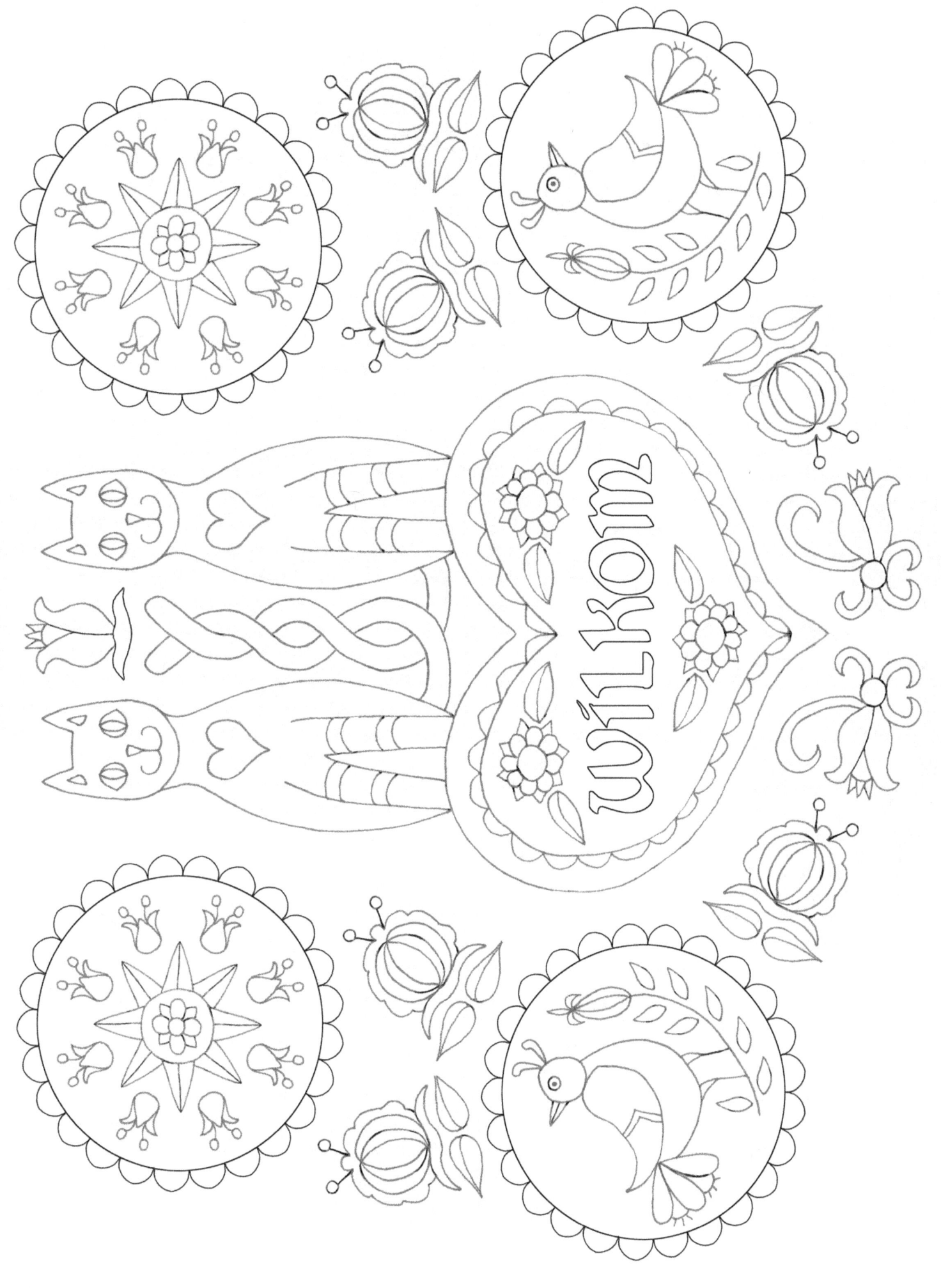

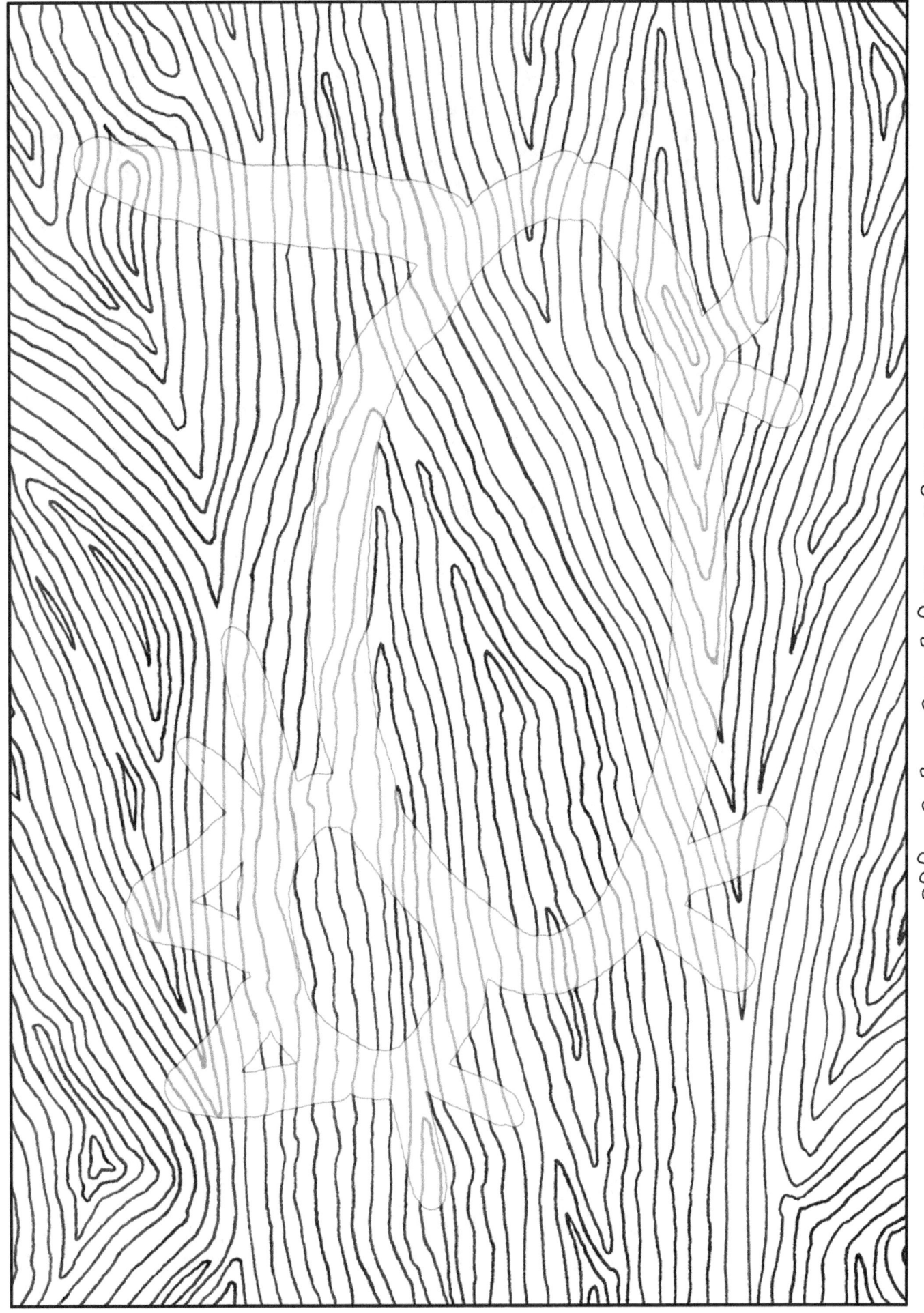

Kind Lady Lives Here

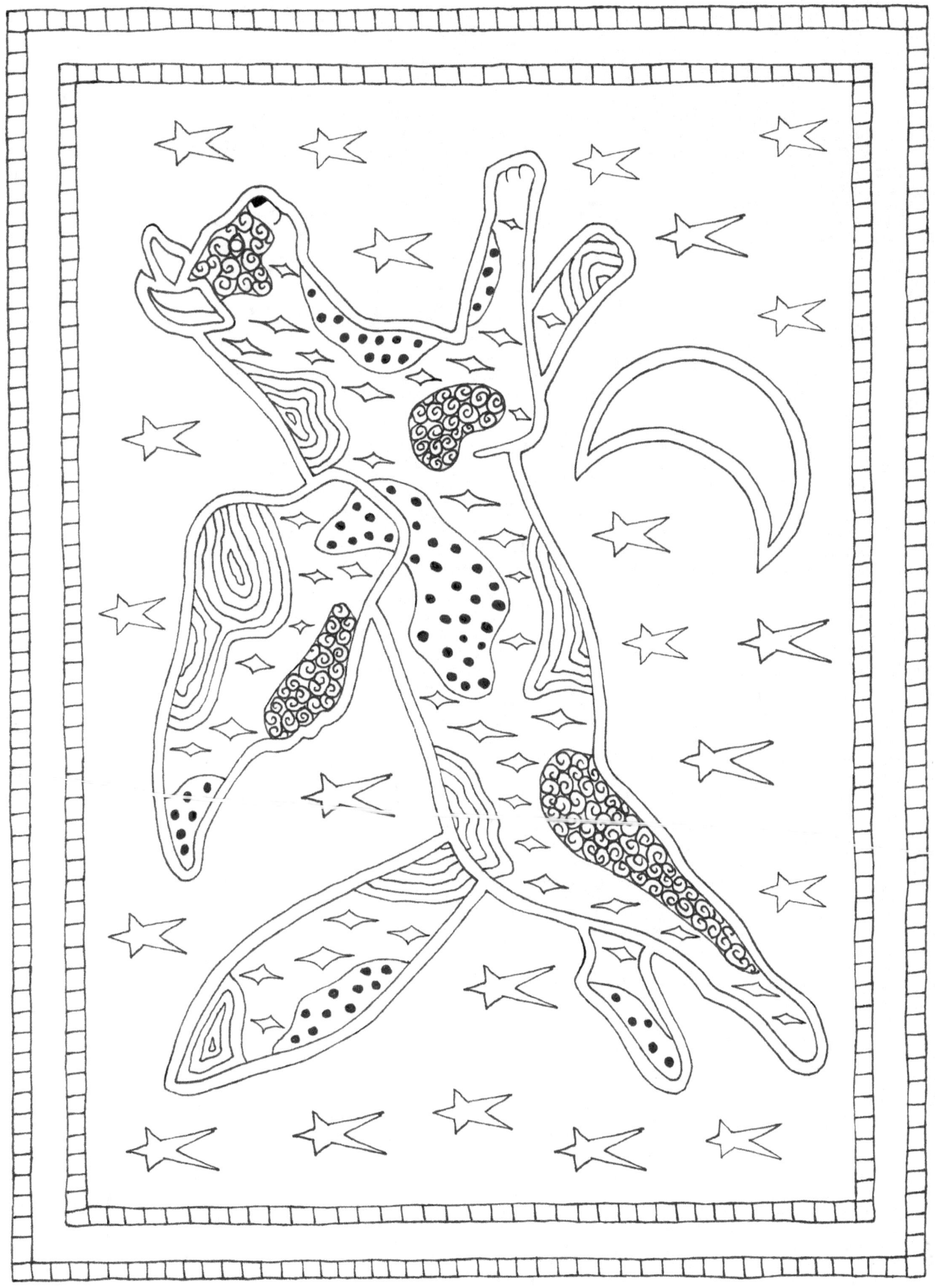